MAKING IT

MAKING IT

How Love, Kindness and Community
Helped Me Repair My Life

JAY BLADES

with Ian Gittins

bluebird
books for life

DISCLAIMER: This is my honest story about how I made it – but I have to consider other people's privacy. A handful of names have been changed in this book, to protect the identities of both friends and enemies.

First published 2021 by Bluebird
an imprint of Pan Macmillan
The Smithson, 6 Briset Street, London EC1M 5NR
EU representative: Macmillan Publishers Ireland Ltd, Mallard Lodge,
Lansdowne Village, Dublin 4
Associated companies throughout the world
www.panmacmillan.com

ISBN 978-1-5290-5919-9 HB
978-1-5290-5921-2 TPB

3 5 7 9 8 6 4 2

A CIP catalogue record for this book is available from the British Library.

Typeset in Fairfield LT Std by Palimpsest Book Production Limited, Falkirk, Stirlingshire
Printed and bound by CPI Group (UK) Ltd, Croydon, CR0 4YY

Contents

Introduction: A repair job   1

1   That Ridley Road Look   5

2   'Have you had your Coon Flakes?'   27

3   The great dressing-gown showdown   52

4   The sins of my father   72

5   A Niagara Falls of lurid orange treacle   87

6   Going forth and multiplying   101

7   Come hell or High Wycombe   121

8   The teaching ability of a peanut   136

9   Lions and Mongolian prisoners   160

10   Urban types collecting stuff like Wombles   183

11   Driving through a tunnel of light   207

12   The *Stig of the Dump* of Wolverhampton   215

13   One big happy family   236

14   *The Repair Shop* is always open . . .   260

Introduction: A repair job

IF YOU HAVE HEARD OF ME, THE CHANCES ARE THAT YOU know me from *The Repair Shop* on BBC1. I'm the jovial geezer in the flat cap who greets nervous visitors when they arrive in our workshop with treasured but damaged family heirlooms for us to repair.

The show has become a phenomenon. It started out tucked away on BBC2 but has now moved to evening primetime on the main channel as millions of viewers tune in each week to watch our team of talented experts restore old chairs, clocks, toys and other much-loved objects in need of a little tender, loving care.

The Repair Shop works so well because it's not just about fixing broken stuff. It's about love, and wonderful family stories, and triggering the precious memories buried deep in those damaged artefacts that can often have both our visitors and us repairers in floods of tears.

1

I am the guy at the front who jollies everyone along and keeps things moving and yet I often tell people that by far the biggest repair job on *The Repair Shop* is me. I must admit I have had some seriously nasty knocks and scrapes along the road to where I am lucky enough to be now.

One thing I have learned from *The Repair Shop* is that everybody – and I mean *everybody* – has an amazing life story. Scratch just beneath the surface and brilliant stories fall out of heroic endeavours, passionate love affairs and vivid experiences that people will never, ever forget.

I'm no different. My story is not unique. I'm not the first, or the last, person to be raised by a single mum, with an absentee father. I'm not the first guy to face racism, to go badly off the rails in his teens, or to have kids before he was ready or mature enough to raise a family.

I've been more than a little bit naughty and I could have turned into a proper wrong 'un, but I'm relieved to say that I managed to turn my life around. And the impulses that helped me to do that are the same ones that power *The Repair Shop* – love, and family, and community.

Before I got into TV, I had another life. Actually, I had a few! I worked with homeless people and with would-be delinquent teenagers. I was a community worker, and a philosophy student. And, after being on the wrong side of the law, I even found myself policing the police!

Like everybody, I've fallen in love and seen relationships go wrong. I've done things that I've been proud of, and made terrible mistakes. I even, not all that long ago, lost my way so catastrophically that I broke down and wondered if I wanted to carry on living at all.

I've found it intense and humbling to revisit my life's

highs and lows for this memoir, but I'm so pleased that I have. With hindsight I can now see that all of these things, good *and* bad, had to happen to me in order for me to finish up where I am now. Where I was destined to be.

There are many ways to make it, and I took the long way around. For a while, I was very broken, but for the last thirty years I have mostly been trying to help people make or repair things. It might be furniture, it might be a relationship: it might even be *themselves*. I love working in *The Repair Shop*, but it is only one element of the many ups and downs of my life story so far.

This is the story of my repair job: of how I made it. I hope that you enjoy it.

1

That Ridley Road Look

LET'S GET THIS STRAIGHT FROM THE START: THIS BOOK is not a misery memoir. It could not be further away from any of that 'Oh, woe is me!' stuff you sometimes read. Whenever I think back on growing up as a little boy, I find a big smile spreading across my face. My childhood was beautiful.

That doesn't mean it was easy. I was brought up by a single mum in Hackney, which people always describe as a 'poor part' of London (although it didn't feel that way to me). We had our hardships, and there were times that we didn't have a lot of food and didn't have a lot of money. But that never stopped me having the time of my life.

My memories of childhood are of playing in the sunshine with my mates; laughs around the estate and in the park; throwing sticks up horse chestnut trees, then using the laces from my shoes to play conkers (I guess I've always been into upcycling!). I remember skipping everywhere. I remember . . . *being happy*.

Which is amazing because, when you look at the circumstances that I was born into, they were not all that promising.

I was born on 21 February 1970 in Edgware General Hospital in Brent, north London, and given the name Jason Willeslie Blades. My mother, Barbara, was just eighteen when she had me. And as soon as she and I were discharged, we went straight to a refuge for the homeless.

How did I come to be starting my life like that? Well, that is quite an interesting story.

My mum was born Barbara Barrow in Barbados and, when she was a little girl, her mum, Ethaline, did what a lot of Caribbean parents did – she left her kids to be cared for by relatives and moved on her own to Britain, to try to make a better life for them. She worked as a nurse in care homes, in Aylesbury, then in London, and sent for my mum when she was thirteen. Mum came over with her younger sister, my Auntie Ann.

My grandmother was by then living with a guy called D'Arcy Blades, who said that he would accept her girls and look after them but only if they changed their surname to his. Thus, as soon as she arrived in England, Barbara Barrow became Barbara Blades.

Mum went to school in Hackney and, a year after she left, she got pregnant with me. My grandmother was by now living with another bloke, who was outraged at Mum being unmarried and pregnant and kicked her out of the house. He laid down the law that she had to go.

What a guy, eh? He was not a nice man. I only ever met

him once, a lot later in my life, and from the second I set eyes on him, I knew: *I do not like you*. My gran didn't even stay with him for all that long. About four or five years later, she moved back to Barbados.

Mum and I fetched up in the homeless refuge for a few weeks and then we stayed with Mum's brother, my Uncle Bertie, in his house in Stoke Newington, in Hackney. Uncle Bertie was there for us when we needed him – which was more than you can say for my dad.

Well, 'dad' sounds the wrong word. I don't even like calling the guy my dad, I prefer to call him The Man Who Contributed Towards My Birth, or TMWCTMB for short, because that is pretty much the sum total of all that he has ever done for me.

I learned in my early twenties that TMWCTMB (don't worry, you'll soon get used to this!) was born in Jamaica and, like my mum, was raised by relatives there for years while his mum made them a life in London. As a lad, I didn't know any of that, or anything about him at all. Nor did I care. He just wasn't around.

I was still a baby when Mum and I moved out of Uncle Bertie's place to a ground-floor council flat a mile away on Cazenove Road, one of the main drags through Hackney. My brother, Justin, came along when I was two. The three of us lived there for the next eight years.

That flat had some pretty funky seventies British décor. When I think back, I remember lots of orange and brown. *Swirly carpets*. Pride of place in the front room went to a giant glass goldfish and a lava lamp. *Cosmic!* I used to love watching the floating shapes shifting in the water in the lamp.

Another thing that fascinated me was the electric meter, in a little box high up on the wall. Every time our lights went out, I'd watch Mum put 50p in. The coin dropping down sounded like music, and then all the lights would come on. It felt like our very own magic box.

Like a lot of Caribbean families, we always had a dried orange peel hanging on a string in the kitchen. It would be the whole peel, cut carefully from the fruit into one long curly strand. It amazed me that Mum could do that. Just try it. It's impossible!

I never asked Mum what the peel was there for, and it was only forty years later that she told me it was medicinal. If Justin or I got poorly tummies, she'd cut a piece off, put it in boiled water and give it to us to drink to settle our stomachs.

I didn't ask her about it when I was a kid, because Mum did not always welcome questions.

My mum was *strict*! You couldn't mess her around. She looked after me and Justin and, as the breadwinner, she put food on the table, but she'd give us a good beating with a belt or stick if we were playing up. She didn't show us a lot of affection.

In fact, the first time Mum told me 'I love you', I was forty years old.

I don't hold this against her. Now I'm older, I can see things were not easy for Mum. She had me when she was eighteen. *What did she know about raising a kid, at that age?* She couldn't even turn to her mum for help, because her step-dad had kicked her out of the house.

I'm sure some therapists might tell me to confront my mum: *'You never gave me love as a kid!'* But what's the point? She did her best. She can't get a time machine, go back to being eighteen and do things differently. I love Mum dearly – and as a boy, although she never said it, I knew she loved me.

Mum went out to work from when Justin and I were very young. An Irish lady who lived around the corner from us would babysit us (and here's a funny story: nearly fifty years later, that lady's daughter introduced herself to me when she came into *The Repair Shop* with an antique saucer!).

Mum worked as a typist on a magazine about African financial affairs. She answered an advert and got the job even though she'd never typed a word in her life. On her first day, she sat looking at a typewriter and a pile of papers without a clue what she was supposed to do.

A woman sitting next to her in the office noticed her confusion. 'Don't you know how to type?' she asked her.

'No!' whispered Mum. 'But I need this job because I've got two kids to feed!'

The woman took pity on her and taught her how to do it. Mum was a quick learner and soon got shit-hot at typing. I remember one time she brought a primitive word processor home to do some work. I stared at the glowing screen in amazement: *Wow! This must be the future!*

But, again, I didn't dare ask Mum any questions about it.

We may have been skint but Mum made us amazing meals. We ate nearly all Caribbean food. I loved one particular dish she made out of corned beef, fried dumplings, onions and chillies. It was poor man's food, but to me it tasted fit for the gods.

Mum also made the best cottage pie I ever tasted – for

a long time, anyway! A few years ago, somebody took me to The Ivy in Covent Garden. I had no idea what a big deal the place was, but they served me up some cottage pie, and it was beautiful! After I'd devoured it, I phoned my mum.

'Mum, I'm sorry to have to tell you this,' I said. 'But I've finally found a place that makes better cottage pie than you . . .'

When I was five, I started at Jubilee Primary School. It's the weirdest thing: I went to this school for four years, and I can hardly recall a single thing about it. I don't remember any friends or teachers whatsoever. I just have a vague recollection of a tiny playground.

In fact, I only have one vivid memory of Jubilee School. My mum came to a parents' evening, looking smart in her business jacket and skirt, and joined in painting pictures with her hands. We had a photo of her holding her hands up, covered in paint. I can still picture that photo.

I'd only just started at Jubilee School when The Man Who Contributed Towards My Birth temporarily reappeared in our lives. Mum was still in touch with him and he told her that he'd like to look after me for a weekend. So, she took me to his flat and left me there.

Weirdly, that weekend is both a blur and a really intense memory for me. There were two girls living in the house – Samantha, who was older than me, and Kara. My dad said they were my sisters, which excited me. TMWCTMB didn't take me back to Mum when he was due to, so she turned up at his door and caused a scene as she took me home.

Mum must have still felt something for my dad then, because he fed her some romantic lines about how we could all live together and be a happy family if she gave him some money to buy us a house. In spite of herself, she believed what he was saying.

She had been saving up. Mum's boss paid her £50 a week, along with a wad of cash that didn't go through the books, so didn't get taxed. She was salting it away, putting it into what was called Partner Hands – a savings scheme between friends and family. A lot of Caribbean expats used to do that.

Mum had saved up £2,000: a shit-load of money back in 1975! She met TMWCTMB on Blackfriars Bridge one lunchtime from her typist job and gave him the money. He immediately vanished, and she didn't hear from him again for months, when all the cash was gone.

As a boy, it didn't bother me that I didn't have a dad. Hardly anybody that I knew had one. Maybe three friends on the entire estate had their dads living with them. In the same way, I never felt poor. We didn't have much money, sure, *but who did?* Everybody was in the same boat!

Instead of a dad, I had loads of caring women around me. Auntie Kate and Auntie Jackie lived down the road from us, in Stamford Hill, and we were always around each other's houses. They were family friends but they were like aunties. Auntie Kate's husband, Uncle Winston, worked at the council baths in Hackney and I used to go swimming there.

Auntie Kate and Auntie Jackie both had a lot of kids. Justin and I played with them every day and called them our cousins: Richard, Ian, Leroy, Tim, Anthony, Philip, Cory, Stacey and Karen. We were all really close. You can tell: more than forty years later, I'm still in touch with all of them.

At Christmas, Mum, Justin and I visited my Auntie Ann in Queen's Park. I got some great presents. One year, I was given an Evil Knievel toy and a Stretch Armstrong figure. *Result!* Stretch was rubber: no matter how hard Justin and I pulled his arms and legs, they wouldn't snap. I hate to think how many toxic chemicals were in there!

Every Christmas, we would get a box of food and presents from Mum's family in Barbados. The second we opened it, the smell from the box was amazing – I'd never even been there but, man, you could *smell* the Caribbean! I get a rush even now thinking about that box.

Like any kid, I loved watching telly. There was a mad show called *The Banana Splits,* and I enjoyed *The Magic Roundabout* and looking through the round window (or would it be the square window today?) on *Play School*. My favourite after-school show was *Michael Bentine's Potty Time* – a comical geezer who pretended to run a flea circus!

As well as kids' programmes, I used to watch a lot of adult sitcoms like *Mind Your Language* and *Love Thy Neighbour*. Today, I can see they were proper racist comedies, but as a lad I didn't realize that. I laughed along. I just enjoyed seeing some black faces on TV. Because there weren't many.

But in the summer, from the age of about seven, as soon as I got home from school I would be playing outside. We had a little patch of grass in the middle of our council estate, like an urban village green, and we'd play there for hours. I'd take root there from teatime until bedtime.

I had to take Justin with me. At two years younger than me, he was my responsibility and I had to look after him while we were playing out. I didn't mind that. We got on

OK, and all my mates and cousins had their own younger brothers and sisters with them as well.

I'd mess around with the other kids. We'd play Kick the Can (hide-and-seek with an extra, can-kicking element built in), rounders and one-touch football. Best of all was British Bulldog, which was trying to run through a line of your mates without being stopped.

We'd go a bit further afield to a local park called Springfield Park, set on a hill, that had swings and slides and a cool roundabout. We used to pick blackberries there. Mum would give me a Tupperware box to put them in, but I'd normally eat them all before I got home.

Justin and I would go up to Stamford Hill to see Auntie Kate and play with our cousins. I remember one boy got given a Chopper bike, which we thought was the best thing ever. He wouldn't let us ride it but we could look at it. On a good day, he'd let us *touch* it.

At those flats was a little old lady called Kitty, who used to sit outside in her wheelchair and watch us play. She'd give us biscuits, which were all stale and rubbery because she never kept them in a tin. We used to sit around her, eat them and pretend to enjoy them to make her happy.

There was a big Jewish community in Stamford Hill and we would see the Orthodox Jewish guys walking around with their black skullcaps and their big bushy beards. They didn't really mix in with other people that much and they all kept themselves to themselves.

We didn't always show them the same respect. We'd sometimes hang out with an older African boy called Rufus, who was a bit too naughty for his own good. He would run to the Jewish guys and push them, or throw stones to try to knock their hats off. He was well out of order.

The Orthodox Jewish guys would lamp him if they caught him but that didn't deter Rufus . . . until the day that he got deliberately run over by a car in Stamford Hill and had to have stitches in his stomach. Rufus told us it was a Jewish guy driving the car. After that, he, and we, gave them a lot more respect.

I remember the Queen's Silver Jubilee in 1977. There were flags all over our estate and big street parties with lots of food. It was so hot! Those parties were the first time I realized that our estate was kind of segregated: all the black people were in one set of flats, and the white folk in another.

That was strange! But, again, I didn't really think anything of it.

Mum was always sending me on errands to the corner shop down the road from the estate. They sold everything. I would take our empty pop bottles to get the 5p deposit on the bottles back, and sometimes Mum would let me spend it on sweets.

One time, she sent me down to buy her some Dr White's. I had no idea that Dr White's were sanitary towels, or even what sanitary towels *were*, but she told me what to ask for in the shop. She said there would be 2p in change and I could spend it on four half-penny Mojos.

Wow! I was over the moon. *Four half-penny Mojos!* I was so happy at this windfall that, on the way back through the estate, I opened up the pack of Dr White's and started throwing them up in the air and catching them. I was chewing my sweets and having the time of my life . . .

Chew! Chew!

Throw! Catch!
Chew! Chew!
Throw! Catch!

Let me tell you, those Dr White's were proper heavy-duty sanitary towels, like little mattresses, but I didn't give a damn! I was strolling along, munching my Mojos, on top of the world . . .

Chew! Chew!
Throw! Catch!

My mum was looking out for me and spotted me, marching across the green where we played, throwing her sanitary towels up in the air. She was *mortified*! Her voice rang out across the estate:

'*Jason!* What the hell are you *doing*? Stop that *right now* and get in here . . .'

When I got indoors, she was furious. I suppose now, I can see why!

On Saturdays, Mum would take Justin and me shopping to Ridley Road Market in nearby Dalston. It was a bustling open-air clothes and fruit-and-veg market but it was a proper endurance test for us, because all we wanted to do was to get home and play outside with our mates.

And that was where Mum first gave me Her Special Look. In fact, I came to think of it as her Ridley Road Look.

We would go to the market and Mum would always bump into Auntie Kate. The two of them would stand and talk . . . and talk . . . and talk. They would normally have seen each other the day before anyway, but that wouldn't stop them gassing for what felt to me like hours.

Justin and I would be stood there, in silence, consumed by boredom. *Come on, Mum! We want to get home and play!*

It was torture – *will they ever stop talking?* – and one Saturday, I couldn't help myself. I clicked my tongue and rolled my eyes in frustration.

Big mistake.

Mum stopped talking for a second. She didn't say anything to me but she gave me a look – a Ridley Road Look – and I knew I was in for it. When we got home, she told me off for how much I had embarrassed her, and gave me beats for being disrespectful to her and Auntie Kate.

That was just how things were. Caribbean parents thought that their children were meant to be seen but not heard. If I was out, playing with my cousins and mates, I was a normal, chatty kid. When I was at an aunt's house, or around grown-ups, I hardly said a word.

It didn't bother me. I was happy. We would go on holiday trips with the other families from the estate. Everybody would chip in to hire a coach, bring along chicken and coleslaw and rice 'n' peas, and off we'd all go, to Margate or even right up to Skegness. We'd always have an amazing time.

Well, nearly always . . .

One time we went on the coach to Littlehampton. It was a boiling hot day and I couldn't cope with the sun. It made me feel sick and my mum got worried about me and took me to the First Aid tent on the end of the pier.

The doctor there took a look at me, and nodded. 'He's got heatstroke,' he said.

Mum could not believe her ears. '*Heatstroke?!* How can he have heatstroke?' she asked the doc. 'He's black! He's supposed to be able to cope with the heat!' But the doctor stood by his diagnosis. I had heatstroke.

We didn't have to go to the seaside to have fun. Auntie Jackie's husband, Uncle Tim, was a taxi driver, and one day he pulled up next to a load of us playing on the grass and said, 'Anybody want an ice cream? If you do, get in!'

We piled into his black cab and he drove us a few streets and got us all ice creams. I hate to think how many kids were crammed into that taxi but Uncle Tim should have got on the phone to the *Guinness Book of Records*! It was such a sweet, simple thing, and more than forty years on, I still remember how happy it made me.

Having no dad, my mum told me from an early age that I was the man of the house. It was weird, in a way. It gave me a double identity. I was a little kid who just wanted to be loved by his mum – but also, *I was the man of the house*! Whatever that meant!

TMWCTMB may have been absent when I was a boy but Justin's dad, whose name was Wayne, was around a bit more. He came and he went. He and I didn't have much to say to each other – as I say, I didn't talk with adults – and we didn't really get on.

I remember one day Wayne came around and was sitting in our front room with his legs wide open, like he was the lord of the manor. He was holding an orange and as I walked in the room, he shouted at me: 'You, boy! Come here!'

I looked all around me. '*Boy*'? Who the hell was '*boy*'?

He beckoned to me: 'Boy! You deaf, or something? Come over here!'

I walked over to him.

'Go to the kitchen and get me a knife to peel this orange!'

I did not like this. I got a sharp knife from the kitchen and walked back over to Justin's dad. Normally, you pass somebody a knife by giving him the handle, but I didn't – I jabbed the blade towards him.

'Here's your knife!' I said.

Wayne started. 'What you doing? Are you trying to stab me?' he asked. He grabbed my hand. 'What's wrong with you?'

'Don't call me "Boy!"' I told him. 'I ain't no "Boy!"'

He looked at me and he laughed. I've never forgotten that. *You are not the man of this house,* I thought. *And you do not call me 'boy'!* For years after that, if anybody ever called me 'boy', I did not react well. At all.

I wasn't sure exactly what being the man of the house meant but I knew it was to do with being responsible and helping to look after Mum and Justin. I had to try to be older than my years at times and pretend to be more grown-up than I was.

It's funny, but being the oldest kid made me think wistfully of my half-sister Samantha, whom I'd met that one day at my dad's house. She was no more than a blurred memory, but in my young mind I looked up to her: *Wow, an older sister! I wish I could get to know her!*

I was a cheerful kid and I didn't really bring any trouble to our house – but Justin was a different matter. My little brother was always up to something and he was one of those kids who always seem to get caught. To be honest, he was a right little terror.

Justin would always be out playing, every evening and every weekend. He never ever sat in the house watching TV, like I sometimes did. That was why it seemed weird, one sunny Saturday afternoon, when he suddenly came darting in the door, ran to our front room and put the telly on.

As Mum and I were looking at him, puzzled, we heard a noise out in the street – sirens. This was a pretty regular sound in Hackney, but we normally heard them racing past our flats. This time, they stopped right outside our front door.

Huh? What was going on?

Mum and I looked out of the window to see three fire engines parked outside our block and yellow-hatted firemen with hoses shouting and running around. And right opposite our building, the row of garages for the estate's residents was ablaze. *Shit!*

It wasn't exactly *The Towering Inferno* but it was a proper full-on fire and Mum and I ran outside to have a closer look. Meanwhile, Justin, the boy who never stayed home, sat indoors watching horse racing on TV.

Horse racing? When had Justin ever liked horse racing?

I had no concrete evidence that Justin had set fire to the garages but, man, it looked pretty suspicious to me! But if it was him, Mum never suspected him and, for once, it meant that he got away with it.

When I was nine, we moved house. Mum managed to replace the cash wasted by TMWCTMB and saved up enough to buy a place. She, Justin and I moved to a semi-detached house a mile away in Londesborough Road, Stoke Newington.

It was a stone's throw from where we had stayed with Uncle Bertie and Auntie Corinne when I was a baby, and we started seeing a lot of them. They were great. Uncle

Bertie was jolly, and Auntie Corinne was so welcoming: she was like a big, warm cake that you could dive into.

Our new place was a lot bigger than the council flat, so Justin and I got our own bedrooms. I remember the head-board of Mum's bed was two huge, outrageous shiny golden circles. I used to walk past her bedroom and gawp in at them. That seventies British décor again!

The new house also had a garden, but the best thing was that just around the corner in the next street was a brick wall with football goals and cricket stumps painted on it. Justin and I spent as much time there with our cousins as we had on the patch of green on the council estate.

The move also meant a change of school. I transferred from Jubilee to Grasmere Primary School, and I loved every minute there. It's such a crazy contrast. Where Jubilee School is just a blank in my memory, I remember everything about Grasmere.

I can still picture the daily walk to school and the uniform of grey shorts and a grey jumper. We had to wear shorts every day of the year, no matter what the weather. I had a friend, Colin James – he was born on the same day as me – who always grumbled about his legs being cold.

'C'mon, Colin, man!' I used to say to him. 'What do you expect? This is *England*!'

On my first day at Grasmere, I also got an inkling that maybe I had not learned all that much at Jubilee. I sat in my class and the teacher told us, 'Today is Monday.' I put my hand up.

'What do you mean?' I asked her.

'You must know the days of the week?' she asked, surprised. 'Monday, Tuesday, Wednesday, Thursday, Friday,

Saturday, Sunday?' I didn't, but I learned them, there and then. God only knows what the teachers must have been doing at Jubilee! Or maybe I just wasn't listening.

Grasmere School was joyous for me. I loved playing in the playground, and the glass of free milk we got each day. I liked calling in to the sweet shop next door after school for penny sweets. But I was a shy kid in the classroom, and I didn't get a lot from the lessons . . . mainly because I couldn't read.

I'd try to focus on a page in a reading book and the letters would dance in front of my eyes. I couldn't begin to make head nor tail of them. I kept my head down, and the teachers didn't seem to notice I was struggling with reading. But it made it hard to learn anything.

I've always been good at adapting and I found ways to sort of cope with not being able to read. But it would be more than twenty years before I got diagnosed as dyslexic – a discovery that changed my life. I just wish that it had come along a lot sooner!

Lessons were a non-starter for me, so it's probably no surprise that my strongest memory of Grasmere is the meals. I absolutely loved school dinners. A lot of people might have written them off as inedible stodge, but I devoured them. *All of them.*

I liked the weird, misshapen, gristly pies they used to give us (although I hate to think what was in them!). I adored the sloppy boiled cabbage that they served with them, and even the spinach. They could give us any old crap at lunchtime and I would wolf it down.

My favourites were the puddings. I couldn't get enough of those chunks of brown sponge slathered in custard. If anybody else was to leave their sponge pudding, I'd be on it in a flash. Mind you, I must admit I drew the line at semolina. *That* was pretty rank.

I rarely got to finish other kids' school meals because the head teacher, Miss Jones, was proper strict like my mum. She used to patrol the lunch hall making sure that every pupil ate up every mouthful of their dinner, whether they liked the food or not.

One day, a kid sitting next to me was struggling badly, and the poor guy puked his meal up all over his plate. Miss Jones had no sympathy for him whatsoever. She just stood next to him, rapped the table, and put his knife and fork back into his hands.

'You've still got to eat your lunch!' she told him. The boy had to finish off the food that he hadn't vomited on.

Blimey! I thought. *That's a bit strong, Miss!*

I qualified for free dinners at school, but it didn't bother me . . . because so did everybody else. We all queued up with our free meal tickets for the dinner ladies, and I felt no shame about being a poor kid. That was just how things were. It was the natural order of things.

I never really had a male role model as a boy – which certainly explains a lot about how I turned out! – but around now was the closest that I came. My mum started seeing a guy called Lloyd MacFarlane and, man, that geezer was *smooth*.

Lloyd was a photographer who also worked as a taxi driver and, let me tell you, he was like no taxi driver you have ever seen before! He was like a black Simon Templar: *The Saint* on TV. I had never seen anyone dress, or speak, or carry themselves the way Lloyd did.

Lloyd was suave and an ultimate charmer but not in a false or a slimy way. He was just a classy guy. He wore hunt shirts and cashmere polo necks. He didn't wear many name brands, or stuff with logos on it, but he always looked immaculate.

And it wasn't just his clobber. Lloyd could talk to anybody, and make anything sound interesting. He was as dapper as Harry Belafonte and then, when he opened his mouth, he was as well-spoken and articulate as Sidney Poitier. He was quiet and didn't say that much, but when he did speak, you *listened*. And you learned something.

Mum saw Lloyd for three or four years and he had a profound effect on me. He was a light-skinned black guy, like me, and I felt proud if people asked me if he was my dad. He was always nice to me – he must have been, because I even didn't mind him being the man of the house for a while!

Lloyd was a sophisticated guy, but I didn't really know anything outside of Stoke Newington and Hackney. Even when Lloyd bought me a racer bike, I didn't really go any further on it than Dalston or Clapton. That bit of turf was my world and I knew it inside-out.

I got a bit more adventurous when I started going to a local adventure playground called Shakespeare Walk. The people who ran it were New Age hippies and they broadened my mind a little – not to mention my palate. They showed us how to make eggy bread. *Eggy bread*? What was *that* all about? But I loved it and I wolfed it down.

The hippy guys used to organize activities and they sent us into London on a Red Rover Adventure. They gave us each a Red Rover all-day bus ticket, and questions to answer: *'How many steps are on the Monument?'* They told us what buses we had to catch to get there.

It was the first time I had been into London and my eyes were on stalks. It was like going travelling! I ran upstairs on the bus and felt as if I was on a plane. I was so excited! *Look – the Tower of London! Big Ben!* I'd been so near to these famous landmarks for years yet I'd never seen them up close before.

That day opened up new frontiers for me, and London buses and, later, Tubes became a major part of my life. Today, in my furniture workshop, I have original metal signs from buses out of Hackney on display on the wall – the 106 and the 253. They mean a lot to me.

Then, when I was ten years old, I went a lot further afield than that – further even than Littlehampton or Skegness! Mum took Justin and me to Barbados to stay with my grandmother, Ethaline, who had gone back to live in the Caribbean a few years earlier.

Going into London was cool but Barbados was a proper adventure. I felt at peace the second that we got there. *It felt like home.* Justin and I loved hanging out on the beach and swimming in the sea. The only problem was getting Mum to actually take us there.

I was well excited to be in the Caribbean, with its turquoise seas and white beaches, but all Mum wanted to do was sit and chat to her mum, Ethaline. I suppose I can see why, as she hadn't seen her in a few years, but if I am honest, I couldn't see the appeal.

My grandmother was not a warm woman. She was very cold and offish. She showed no interest at all in her grand-kids, and the way she looked at me always made me worry,

Uh-oh – what have I done wrong? Have I done something to annoy you? I don't think I ever saw her smile.

I reckon my grandmother's remote nature shaped my own upbringing. She never showed any affection to my mother when she was a child, and that rubbed off and affected the way that Mum treated me. *Who knows?* I just knew I didn't want to be around Granny if I could help it.

Despite this, she and Mum talked for hours in her front room as Justin and I sat itching to get to the beach. They were going on and on about old times and I was thinking, *come on, Mum, I have nothing to do with these old times – let's go!*

It was Ridley Road Market all over again, and I was so impatient that I earned myself a couple of Ridley Road Looks. And then, when we finally made it to the beach, I got heatstroke again!

When we got back to London, something important happened. I guess I might as well confess this upfront, because it is going to form quite a major theme of this life story: *I have always had an eye for the ladies.* And, at the grand old age of eleven, I got myself my first girlfriend.

I had known Tracy Powell when I lived in Cazenove Road. She had loads of brothers, and we all used to mess around and play together. Then, when I moved up to Londesborough Road, she started coming up on her own to see me.

Tracy was a bit of a tomboy. She was always up for climbing trees and when we were little, she was just like one of the boys, really. She was a good fighter and could look after herself. But one day, when the two of us were hanging out, she told me, 'You can kiss me, if you want to.'

Wow! Really? I was just getting to the right age where I was extremely excited to hear words like that! So, from that point on, Tracy and I did a lot less climbing trees, and a lot more kissing. I must say, it felt to me like a definite upgrade in our activities.

Adolescent flings like that rarely last, but after the kissing stopped, I always stayed in touch with Tracy. I kept, and treasured, a photo of me and her standing by Lloyd's car, outside the Londesborough Road house. When she died from cancer, just a few years ago, I was gutted.

Tracy was so cool, and I think that in many ways, for me, she set the benchmark for all of my future girlfriends. For years afterwards, I was always looking for the same thing in a woman – a good mate that I could also kiss. Even if we didn't climb any trees!

Yet despite my eye for the ladies kicking in, I was still basically a kid. I was still enjoying my happy-go-lucky childhood, having laughs with my mates, playing table tennis down the youth club, going swimming, or just messing about in the park. Life was good. I was still *innocent*.

That all changed the day that I walked through the gates of secondary school.

2

'Have you had your Coon Flakes?'

As a confident kid, I wasn't at all intimidated about starting secondary school. I had had a joyful time at Grasmere Primary, and I assumed Big School would be just as cool. My only concern was that it might not have a sweet shop next door, as Grasmere did.

I soon realized that I should have been a lot more worried than I was.

I'd had a lot of friends at Grasmere but we all went separate ways. Most kids stayed in our area and went on to schools in Homerton or Hackney Downs, but my mum sent me to Highbury Grove School, on the way to Islington. She'd heard the teaching was good there.

I'll never forget getting my uniform before starting there. I had grown interested in clothes from seeing how well Lloyd dressed, how great he always looked and the respect he got for it. When I was ten, I had been given a beautiful cashmere sweater, and it was my pride and joy.

Mum put it in the washing machine and it shrunk until it looked like Action Man's jumper! I was horrified and asked her never to wash my clothes again. From that day, I washed and ironed them all myself. I got shit-hot at ironing (too good, because soon Mum had me ironing all of her pleated crêpe work skirts. They were a nightmare!).

We got given vouchers to buy my school uniform from John Lewis. I'd never even *heard* of John Lewis, but when we went in the store, and I felt the quality of the shirts and jumpers, I knew, *Shit, man, this is good stuff!* I went off for my first day at Highbury Grove feeling well dapper.

One pal from Grasmere who did go to the new school with me was a smart, gentle little Indian guy called Iqbal. We were only eleven and both still quite small, skinny kids, but there were a lot of older, tougher boys at the new school who quickly turned their attention to us.

Right from the first few days, a gang of eight or ten white boys, aged fifteen or so, would surround Iqbal and me at playtime. They'd sneer at us, or push us, and say things I didn't really understand.

'Eh, wog a matter?' they'd ask me. 'What did you have for breakfast this morning – Coon Flakes? Or Wog-a-Bix?' Then they'd laugh. They'd call me 'nigger', a word that I had honestly hardly ever heard before.

At first, I didn't take it that seriously and thought it was just older-kid humour. But then they started hitting and kicking us. I would always push and slap them back but Iqbal was timid and used to just take it. I'd try to defend him but he got some bad beats and he'd end up crying.

I didn't realize how bad it all was until I'd been there a couple of weeks and I was hanging out and sitting on a wall near my house with a bunch of cousins and mates after school. I decided to try to make them laugh.

'Hey, what did you have for breakfast this morning?' I asked. 'Did you all have Wog-a-Bix?'

Every head swivelled towards me. They all stared at me.

'*What* did you say?' one of them asked.

'Or did you niggers have Coon Flakes?' I continued.

Why weren't they laughing?

'Jay, why are you saying these things? Those are not nice names, man!' They all looked proper shocked.

'It's what some of the kids at school say to me,' I said. 'And they hit me, and beat up my friend Iqbal.'

One of my mates, Clifton, was an older lad, sixteen or so, who had already left school – in fact, I think he had been kicked out. You didn't want to cross Clifton, and right now he was looking pretty cross himself.

'I'm coming to your school tomorrow, Jay,' he said. 'And you are going to point out to me who is calling you these things.'

'OK,' I agreed.

I have no idea how he got in, but the next morning Clifton was waiting in the school playground when the bell went for break. 'Who is it, then?' he asked me.

'It's him, him, him and that one . . .' I said, pointing out my usual gang of tormenters lurking a little way away. Clifton marched over to them.

'Why do you call Jay bad names?' he asked.

I was too far away to hear the answer, but whatever it was, Clifton didn't like it, because a second later he was laying into them. They must have outnumbered him eight-to-one but it made no difference. He smashed them up and they ran off in different directions.

'If any of them call you those names again, Jay, let me know,' he said as he left. 'And I'll come back.'

Well, Clifton was trying to help, and he probably thought his intervention had solved my bullying problem, but it actually had the direct opposite consequence. He had beaten up some of the school's top dogs and *they weren't having that*. The problem was that I had to go to school again the next day, and the day after, when Clifton wasn't there, and now there weren't just eight kids trying to smack me about at playtime.

There were twenty.

It was the start of a seriously bad time for me and Iqbal. I'd still do my best to fight back but Iqbal was always passive and got treated like a punchbag. The white kids' speciality was breaking his glasses. He had to tape them back together at home every night.

It was my introduction to racism and it was *nasty*. Before I went to Highbury Grove, I was colour-blind. I was raised in the ghetto, sure, but everyone was mixed in together: black, white, Asian, Turkish, Chinese. I never even saw skin colour. We all had a brilliant time together.

Now, I realized for the first time that the colour of my skin was a big problem for some people. Because they just didn't like black people.

In fact, having never known racism existed before, I suddenly became super-aware of it. It was an overnight awakening. I began to take note of the way that black people were shown on TV, in shows that before then I had happily watched without being bothered.

There was a racist comedian, Bernard Manning, telling jokes about 'wogs' and 'Pakis'. There was Jim Davidson, doing a stupid voice for his black alter ego, Chalkie White. And as for *The Black and White Minstrel Show* . . . what the hell was *that* about?

I had always felt like I belonged in England – like it was my natural home. Now, suddenly, I wasn't so sure.

There was some TV that spoke to me. A few years earlier, I had watched *Roots* on TV on Sunday nights with my mum. I was a bit too young to *get* it then, but now the story of Kunta Kinte, the African boy captured and sold into slavery, hit me like a hammer.

Shit! Was that what they used to do to black people? It made me super-angry: *This stuff happened all those years ago*, I thought, *and it's still going on now!* In terms of understanding racial injustice, it was a real fire-starter for me.

My life had been about skipping to the park, and Kick the Can, and picking blackberries, and Mojo chews. Now, suddenly, I woke up to another side of life: to bigotry, and violence, and racism. I had gone to Highbury Grove a happy, innocent little boy.

That innocence was about to get beaten right out of me.

When the bullying at school started, I tried to tell the teachers about it. One morning after playtime, we were standing in line to go back in class. I was bleeding from a cut to my face and Iqbal's glasses were smashed again. I stepped out of the line and spoke to the teacher.

'Sir, some boys hit us in the playground,' I told him.

'They punched me in the face, and broke Iqbal's glasses, and . . .'

'Shut up and get back in the line! *Now!*' the teacher told me. He just did not want to know. They never did.

I was trying to stand my ground but the bullies were a lot bigger than me and I got some bad licks. After one particularly bad day, I got home in tears. My mum saw me and asked me what was wrong.

'A boy in school hit me in the playground,' I sniffed. Mum stared at me.

'Well, why didn't you hit him *first?*' she asked.

Those words hit home. I took serious note of them.

I would have liked to talk to Lloyd, and ask his advice . . . but he wasn't around any more. One day, he had just gone. Mum never told me why, or where, and she and I didn't exactly have the kind of relationship where I could quiz her in detail about her romantic life. But I missed him.

One day, I was walking down a corridor at school. I saw Iqbal with his back to me. He had his head down and was fiddling with something.

'Hey, Iqbal! You OK?' I asked him.

He turned around. I saw the tearstains on his face. 'Jay, I can't fix them,' he said.

'Fix what?'

Iqbal held his glasses out to me. They were only NHS specs, and the bullies had smashed them so many times that there was more Sellotape on them than there was glass or frame. And now there was no room for any more.

'I can't fix them this time,' he said.

It was heart-breaking. I knew Iqbal's family were poor,

like mine, and they couldn't afford to buy him new specs. Even now, forty years on, I choke up at the memory of that poor, sweet kid holding out his ruined glasses. He looked so forlorn – so unhappy.

I looked at Iqbal, and something in me *snapped*. It clicked into place.

Those fuckers are not going to get away with this!

From that day, I changed. I just wasn't going to stand for this shit any more. These bastards weren't going to bully me, or anybody else. If they wanted a fight . . . I was going to give them one.

If anybody pushed me, or hit me, or called me a racist name now, I was going to have them. No question. No quarter. And that didn't just go for me. If those bullies went for Iqbal, or other vulnerable kids, well, I would make that my business as well:

'Oi! Leave him alone! If you want a fight, *I'll* fight you – now!'

And that became what I did at school. *I fought*. Every day. And, if you do something every day, you get very good at it. I got very, very good at fighting.

I took my cue from my mum's words: '*Why didn't you hit him first?*' If there was any trouble brewing around me in the playground – and there normally *was* – then I was ready for it. And my calling card was instant mega-violence.

There is a ritual to a fight starting, in school or a pub or anywhere. It normally kicks off with a load of trash-talking and posturing. A guy will say something, then his adversary will say something back:

'*What are you looking at?*'

'*Who wants to know?*'

'*I want to know!*'

They will square up to each other for a slanging match and do a bit of pushing and shoving. It's a minute or two before the first punch gets thrown. Most of the time, there ends up being no fight at all.

'*Right, let's have it!*'

'*Yeah? Come on, then . . .*'

Well, I didn't bother with any of that. '*Why didn't you hit him first?*' If anybody came up to me in the playground, or gave me a dirty look, or *especially* if they called me 'wog' or 'coon'. . . I was at them. *Instantly.*

It gave me the element of surprise. A big kid coming up to a little lad and taunting him does not expect the nipper to smash him in the face a split second later. But that was what I did. There was no preamble from me. No foreplay. As soon as it started, I'd go for it. *Bang!*

Get your retaliation in first!

My technique was to go for the bullies' faces and wallop them until they backed off. If they got me on the floor – and they often did – I'd grab them by the balls. As soon as I'd whacked them *there*, they were bent double and, well, knackered.

Or I would pretend that they had hurt me and I'd stay down. The older kids were pretty stupid. They would turn around to their mates, smiling in triumph, thinking they'd won – '*Ha! He's supposed to be a tough guy?*' – and I'd jump up and smack them one.

There were no rules. I would do whatever it took.

I went to school to fight, and I fought every day. Some

days, other little kids would come to me bleeding or crying. They would tell me who had hurt them and I'd take off around the playground like an Exocet missile, looking for revenge. I'd normally get it.

I didn't always win. I wasn't a superhero, or Muhammad Ali, and some days I'd get a bad beating. But soon I was winning a lot more fights than I was losing. I earned myself a reputation – and the sad thing was, *I got to love fighting.* You always love what you are good at.

It was funny – the kids would pay me in puddings! I still loved school-dinner sponge pudding and custard, and the kids I'd saved from the bullies would give me theirs to thank me. Some days, I'd be sitting at the table with six puddings in front of me like King Henry VIII!

I toughened up at that school good and proper. I had walked through the gates a wide-eyed little boy but in no time, I was street and savvy. I picked up other bad habits alongside the fighting: by the time I was twelve, I was a seasoned cigarette-smoker (not at home, though!).

The playground violence kept me busy but, in the classroom, I was not doing well. Nobody had even heard of dyslexia in those days, so when I still couldn't read as I entered my teens, the teachers just assumed I was thick. They wrote me off.

My school split each year into three streams: the Ps, the Ms and the Ls. I still don't know what they stood for, but we used to call them the Perfects, the Mediums and the Learners – or probably it should have been the *Losers.* The brainy pupils like Iqbal were in the Ps.

The funny thing was that I started off in the Ps. *God knows why!* It lasted for two days, until the teachers got around to asking me some questions, at which point they dropped me to the Ms. I hardly even touched the sides there: a week later, I was down in the Ls.

The L lessons were licensed anarchy. I'd walk in the class to find yelling and missiles flying about everywhere. Most days, the teacher might as well not have been there. There were a lot of very, very naughty kids in the Ls. I quickly became one of them.

I didn't learn a single thing and I didn't expect to. In the Ls, we all knew we weren't going to get academic qualifications or go off to university. We didn't care. I would turn up to school every day to fight and to get a free dinner. That was all I was bothered about.

The one lesson that I liked was drama. I enjoyed acting, and the young teacher was really pretty so we all tried to impress her. Drama was the only class where we L kids behaved properly, but the only reason for that was that we fancied the teacher.

Sport has never been my thing but, as I got into my teens, I sprang up and suddenly became really tall. This was very good for my fighting, and in PE at school I got brilliant at playing defence in basketball and blocking the other team's shots.

My PE teacher was so impressed that he sent me off for trials for the England youth basketball squad. But I had to go on my own on a Tube to Morden, right on the other side of London. When I got there, I didn't know anybody and I felt out of place. I soon dropped it.

My constant battles in the playground were getting me into trouble with the teachers, and they called my mum up to the school a couple of times to talk to her. I hadn't told

Mum much about the hard times I was having there. It was one of the many things we just didn't talk about.

She didn't really know about what was going on, so she told my class teacher: 'If Jason is playing you up, you must sort him out! Discipline him!' Unknowingly, Mum had gave the staff *carte blanche* to go hard on me. They took full advantage.

The routine was that if I was talking in class, or answering back, the teacher would send me to the house master. This guy had a plimsoll with the top elastic band missing, and he'd bend me over and give me some hard whacks. Always fifteen of them, for some reason.

If the house master wasn't satisfied, he'd forward me to the deputy headmaster, who would tell me to stick my hands out and get his cane out. *Swish! Swish! Swish!* Three swipes on each hand; six of the best. *Ow!* He wanted it to hurt, and would look at me to make sure it had.

I was too stubborn to react, and if I managed not to flinch from the pain – even if my palms were coming up in welts – the deputy head would send me to the headmaster. Shit, *there* was a man who knew all about caning little boys! I used to dread being sent to him.

Sometimes, the staff would mete out their own direct punishment to us L kids without feeding us into the caning system. I remember once I was talking in the back row of a social studies lesson. The teacher heard me and came marching over to me.

'Shut up, Blades!' he told me. 'And stand up!'

I did, and the guy punched me hard in the stomach, twice – *WALLOP! WALLOP!* – like he was a heavyweight boxer. I was bent over, winded, and blinking back tears as he strolled back to the front of the class and carried on teaching as if nothing had happened. As if he hadn't just beaten up a child.

The teachers at Highbury Grove were all white except for one black guy, who was the biology teacher. I had no contact with him: he only taught the P and M streams. The school clearly saw no point in teaching us L kids about biology.

The violence, and the racism, and the unfairness changed me as a person. In just a few weeks, I stopped being that happy, carefree little lad and grew really angry at the world. I became proper hot-headed, and on a hair trigger to attack anybody who antagonized me.

In no time, I was notorious for my temper and explosions of violence – '*Don't fuck with Jay Blades!*' – and it earned me enemies. There were two mostly all-white council estates in Hackney, the Packington and the Marquess, and some kids from there hated me for my attitude.

Because I loved my food so much, I often used to eat my school dinner – plus my extra puddings – and then go to the chip shop for a bag of chips. One day, I was heading across the playground to do just that when a mate ran up and stopped me.

'Jay, you can't go out!' he said.

'What do you mean, I can't go out?'

'The Packington and the Marquess have come down for you, and they want your blood. Look!'

I looked where he was pointing. Outside the school railings were a load of white kids, staring and pointing at me. Some were in the National Front uniform of skinheads and red braces. I can still picture that one of them was carrying a harpoon gun.

Wow! Shit!

The school caretaker had got wind that something was up, and he had come down, locked the gates and put chains across them to avoid a riot in the playground. But it shows how angry and messed up I was that, if he hadn't done that, I'd have run out and started laying into them.

It would not have been clever. I would have got a serious kicking. But I just did not give a fuck.

By now, the violence was not restricted to school for me. Everywhere that I went around east London, I constantly had to be looking over my shoulder. It was proper unhealthy. I knew there were a lot of guys out there who hated me, and I hated them back.

I'm not denying that I got a bit naughty. I had a reputation around the manor and, when you have a rep, there are always people who want to come and challenge you. Some of my mates began refusing to come out with me because they knew the evening would end up in a fight.

Some of it was personal but a lot of it was racism, pure and simple. The National Front were big news back then and you had to be wary of them. Weirdly, there used to be two local black twins who used to run with the NF and hand out flyers for them. *That* blew my mind!

Yet you knew where you stood with the National Front and with out-and-out racists. If I ran into them, and they called me a wog or the N-word, we had a ruck, and that was it. I got more pissed off by people being nice to my face then racist behind my back. It was harder to deal with.

And the biggest danger of all were . . . *the police.*

I admit we brought a bit of trouble with the police on ourselves. I was still hanging around the streets with my mates after school, including Clifton, who had come up to my school and beaten up the bullies. And Clifton had got his own special superpower.

We would all be sitting in on a wall chatting and Clifton would spot a bobby on the beat minding his own business, a good hundred yards away. 'Watch this!' Clifton would say, and pick a big stone up off the ground. We all knew what was coming next.

Clifton would take aim and whang the rock through the air. *Whoomph!* Nine times out of ten he would hit the copper's helmet and knock it right off his head. We would all be cracking up . . . until the policeman saw us.

'*Oi! Come here!*'

Then it would be Benny Hill-chase time as we all scattered in different directions as the copper chased us and radioed for reinforcements. It was crucial that we got away – because if we didn't, we knew we would get as bad a kicking from them as we would from the NF.

There's no easy way of saying this: a lot of police in the eighties did not like black people. I know people say nowadays that the Met Police in London are systemically racist – well, it was a whole load worse back then! A lot of police were racist and didn't even bother trying to hide it.

They'd use and abuse the notorious 'sus law', which allowed them to stop and search anybody they suspected had done something bad, or might be about to do something bad, or they just didn't like the look of. We got used to that. It became a predictable routine.

We'd go to our youth club after school and kids, or even elders who were coming to talk to us, would turn up bruised and beaten because the police had given them a doing over. The youth workers would fix them up the best they could.

My bit of London was a simmering pot and sometimes it boiled over as tensions and frustrations exploded. When I was thirteen, I saw rioting at first hand after Colin Roach, a twenty-one-year-old black guy, died in custody at Stoke Newington Police Station.

No police got charged over his death. We never thought they would.

The injustice burned away at us. A year or two after it came out, I saw a film called *Babylon*. Set in Brixton, it starred Brinsley Forde, from the reggae group Aswad, as a young guy battling everyday racism, the NF and police brutality. It spoke to us because that was our lives.

I started seeing myself in terms of my blackness. Despite having no interest in sport, I began to follow the West Indies cricket team like our elders did. They were great. They were the best team in the world – *Clive Lloyd! Viv Richards!* – and they always kicked England's ass.

My life was full of conflict but I mostly managed to avoid direct dealings with the police. I knew there was nothing to gain from it, and I was too speedy for them to catch me when Clifton knocked their helmets off. Sometimes, though, I just had no escape.

One night about ten o'clock, I was mooching back to Londesborough Road from the park when a police van pulled up next to me. A flat-cap officer with a big bushy black beard got out of the front passenger seat and called me over.

'Oi! You! I want a word with you!'

I walked over.

'Where've you been? What you been doing?'

'Nowhere,' I said. 'Nothing. I'm just on my way home.'

'I don't believe you. We're gonna search you. Get in the van!'

The back doors swung upon and the black-bearded copper shoved me inside. There were five or six uniformed policemen sitting in the van waiting for me. They didn't even bother to search me. They just beat the shit out of me.

It was brutal. They were laying into me with fists, feet and truncheons, and all I could do was roll into a ball on the floor of the van and wait, *pray*, for it to end. It probably lasted two minutes but it felt a lot, lot longer as their mocking laughter echoed around the van.

'This'll show you! Black bastard!'

When they had had enough, they chucked me out and drove off. I staggered home to inspect my latest black eye and bruises. I didn't tell Mum how I'd got them. She tended to worry – and Justin normally gave her plenty enough to worry about. She didn't need more hassle.

That big-bearded sergeant was a psycho. We called him Blackbeard and avoided him at all costs. He'd drive around in the evenings, with his unit, looking for black youths to beat up. Afterwards, he'd dump us in a white area like Millwall so we might get a second kicking on the way home.

Fortunately, it only happened to me one more time. But a few of my mates were not so lucky and became regular targets for them.

It was all horrific. I knew the racism was wrong. I knew the sus laws were wrong. I know the police brutality was wrong. And I knew that we could do fuck-all about any of it. It all added to my constant, burning sense of injustice.

Thankfully, there was also a lighter side to my life. In my early teens, I got big into music. As a kid, I could always tell what mood Mum was in by the music she played in the kitchen on Saturdays. If it was 'Misty Blue' by Dorothy Moore, I knew she was in a certain mood and I should stay away because she'd probably just got her heart broken again.

There was always music around in Stoke Newington. A pub called The Nevill Arms had blues parties, with music blasting out through the open door. I used to love hanging around outside listening to it and then, when I got a bit older, sneaking in.

I got more heavily into music through a mate at school called Jonathan Joseph. Jonathan was a smart kid, a 'Perfect' in the P stream, but he and I hit it off from the start and hung out a lot together. He used to do mixing and we'd go to youth clubs and parties together.

Jonathan was to do super-well for himself. He went on to become DJ Spoony, first on pirate radio and Kiss FM, and then at the BBC on Radios 1 and 2. In fact, I was the guy who initially christened him Spoony, because I said that his legs bent outwards like a pair of spoons!

My first musical love was reggae. I liked soul music, but it was reggae that really got my heart beating and fed my soul: it still is. I couldn't get enough of the classic roots-reggae artists like Bob Marley, Alton Ellis and John Holt. I loved their mix of love and social rebellion.

Spoony and I began going to blues and reggae parties in a Methodist church in Stoke Newington, and to sound clashes in a local community centre, Homerton House, to hear sound systems like Kilimanjaro, Saxon and Coxsone, up from south London. You could buy cassettes by those guys. I still have some of them.

We would go further afield, to house parties in Tottenham that we used to call 'big people raves', where DJs like the young Trevor Nelson would be playing. One of our favourite places was Caxton House in Islington. They had some great parties there.

Like any lairy teenager, I got into drinking. Going out at weekends, I'd knock back Cherry B, Lambrini and Babycham. I tried a heavy-duty lager called Gold Label, which was pretty lethal stuff. But I met my match when somebody gave me Thunderbird.

Thunderbird is a strong fortified wine and I was drinking it one Saturday afternoon when I was fourteen and raving at Homerton House. I had drunk a whole bottle of the stuff and was sitting on the steps outside of the centre when it dawned on me that I was out of my tree.

A friend realized I was in a state and got me some food: 'You need to soak up the drink, Jay!' He gave me a Jamaican patty and some corn on the cob. I managed to work my way through the patty but I dropped the corn cob on the floor.

I was sitting, swaying, on the steps trying to pick up that corn but, man, it was dodging me! I was scrabbling for it for ages. I could hear people laughing at me. Then my mate came back: 'Shit, don't eat that off the floor, bruv! That's *disgusting!*'

I hated it. I didn't like feeling so out of control, so I knocked drinking on the head. It was the same story with cannabis. Like any Hackney kid, I smoked spliff in my early teens. We'd go down to the local frontline, in Dalston, and buy a little £3 bag of weed. Or, if we were flush, £5.

That was until the day that I went down to a local youth club with a few friends after school. We found it closed up, and we didn't know why. Our gang elected me to go inside and ask the elders what was going on and when it would be opening up.

There must have been some very *progressive*, let's say, youth workers there, because one of them rolled me a spliff and said she'd be back to talk to me in a minute. I sat and smoked the joint and chilled out, she came back ten minutes later, then I went back out to rejoin my pals.

Well, that was what I thought. The reality was rather different.

'Jay, where have you been, man?' one of them asked me. 'You were in there for two hours!'

'Eh? You're crazy! I was there for ten minutes!'

'Are you joking us? It was two hours!' I checked my watch. *Shit!* They were right. I had lost all track of time as I sat and puffed myself into a stoned stupor. I still felt weird and messed up in my head all the next day in school.

So, I gave up the spliff as well. It wasn't a moral choice: I just could not risk being that out of it. While I was that vulnerable, anybody could do anything to me and, with my rep, I knew that I needed to have my wits about me when I was out and about.

I had to be careful where I went. When I walked to school, if I stayed on the main drag through Stoke Newington and up to Highbury Grove, I was OK. But if I veered off the beaten track, and went to places outside of that, it would lead to trouble.

My friends and I went around in a crew because that was how we liked it, and also because there was safety in numbers. I knew for a fact that if I ever walked to Islington on my own, I'd get spat on. And it wasn't just National Front skinheads – ordinary-looking geezers would do it.

So, we all looked after and looked out for each other, and the only time I was ever really walking around the streets on my own was if I was going off to meet a girl.

Unfortunately, by now, I was going off on my own to meet girls *a lot.*

If my eye for the ladies had kicked in at eleven, by the time I was in my mid-teens I was on heat. I had hit puberty and my hormones were going mental. Sure, I was going to blues parties with my best mate Spoony to hear the music . . . but I was also always on the lookout to pick up a nice girl.

I wasn't shy about chatting up the girls at Homerton House and Caxton House. That was what *I* was there for and *they* were there for. I'd try to feed them my best lines – well, whatever best lines you can have, when you're fourteen. If they let me walk them home, fantastic!

I would go up to the Holly Street Estate in Dalston to check out the girls, which was a bit of a no-no. The guys on the estate didn't like it: *What, that lippy nutter from Stoke Newington is coming up here after our girls?* I had a couple of run-ins and it made Holly Street a no-go area for me.

Except that I ignored the danger and I still went.

I became a bit of a player. Once, I found myself going out with two sisters at the same time. *God only knows how I thought they wouldn't talk to each other and they wouldn't find out!* When the penny dropped for them, their cousin hunted me down to sort me out.

46

The cousin was one of the top boys in Stoke Newington and his name was Winston Silcott. He found me and gave me a slap. And, if you think that name sounds familiar, you're right, because a year later he became a figure of national infamy. A public hate-figure.

When the Broadwater Farm riot kicked off down the road in Tottenham in 1985, Winston Silcott was one of three men who went to jail for the murder of PC Keith Blakelock (although his conviction was later quashed). Another of the guys who was jailed, then later had his conviction overturned, was Mark Braithwaite. I knew him a little bit, too, because his dad had used to date my mum.

So, given the trouble that my raging libido was getting me into around the streets of east London, it was probably just as well that I now got myself a steady girlfriend.

Her name was Maria, and she was a beautiful mixed-race girl who was two years older than me. I used to notice her walking around Stokie – all the guys did! She was what we used to call a round-the-way girl, which basically meant that all the men wanted to get with her.

Maria looked out of my league – she looked out of *everybody's* league! – but, for better or worse, I've always been pretty brazen when it comes to talking to the ladies. I took a deep breath, figured *nothing ventured, nothing gained*, and asked her if she'd like to go out with me.

Mind you, I was proper surprised when she said yes!

Maria was cool. She'd been a tomboy when she was younger, like Tracy Powell, but now she'd grown out of that and was a real lady and very feminine. I quickly got really serious about her – as I demonstrated by making a major artistic and home-décor commitment.

To go with my reggae and soul, by the mid-eighties I was getting into hip-hop, both the music and the graffiti side of things. A huge, gentle guy at school called Russell Fraser was in the L-stream classes with me. He was well over six feet tall, loved rap and graffiti, and was a street artist.

Russell had all these notebooks that he used to fill up with amazing drawings, and one day I was flicking through them when I saw one that I loved. It was a big love heart with ribbons coming out of it. *Ting*! A lightbulb came on over my head: *I want that on my bedroom wall!*

Mum was strict in many ways but she was surprisingly cool with this plan, so Russell came around with his paints and spray cans and graffitied my bedroom wall. On the ribbons it said 'JAY' and 'MARIA' and underneath it said 'LOVE FOREVER'. It looked like 3D! It was beautiful.

The fact that I was now with Maria didn't mean my local enemies had forgiven me all of my earlier crimes of going after girls from their estates. They still wanted payback, and when I had just turned fifteen, I had one of the most terrifying experiences of my life.

I was going with about ten mates to a funfair, about a mile away in Shoreditch. The fair was in sight and we were walking down the street towards it when a guy that I knew came running towards me.

'Jay, you've got to go!' he told me. 'Holly Street are here!'

'Yeah?' I said, full of bravado. 'So what?'

'No, Jay, you don't understand – *all* of Holly Street are here!'

I heard somebody next to me mutter: 'Bloody hell! Look!'

I looked down the street. Led by a guy called Fiddles, who really did *not* like me at all, at least a hundred Holly

Street Estate kids were heading towards us. *Shit!* I had recently seen the film *Gremlins*, and this looked like the scene when all the gremlins first appeared!

I glanced around me. My army of ten mates had suddenly reduced to three. The rest had scarpered, sharpish. But Spoony's brother, whom we used to call Milky because he was smooth with the ladies, was still there.

'What we gonna do, Jay?' he whispered.

Now, I was an aggressive kid. I had launched myself into way too many fights where the numbers and the odds had been against me. I was so hardened to violence by now that I didn't really get scared before fights – but, right now, *I was shit-scared*. There was only one thing for it.

'RUN!' I yelled.

We turned and we legged it. I heard a battle cry from Fiddles – 'Get 'im!' – and the Holly Street boys came chasing after us. *Shit!* I had no doubt at all that, if they caught us, I was in for the kicking of my life.

The three of us charged full pelt through the streets and round corners, with the mob in hot pursuit. More through panic than strategy, we split up, and I suddenly found myself alone, in a side street, knowing that my enemies were a hundred yards behind me at most.

If I just kept running, eventually some of them would catch me. There were just too many of them! I had to hide!

There was a van parked by the side of the road next to me. I dropped down and rolled under it. Ten seconds later, my army of pursuers turned into the street and sprinted along it. They sounded like a herd of cattle stampeding.

'Where is the bastard?'

'Where did he fucking go?'

Jesus! I felt sure they would hear my heart beating as I lay perfectly still under the van. It felt as if the crowd was running past me for days. After their thudding footsteps vanished into the distance, it was ten minutes before I felt safe enough to come creeping out.

I couldn't believe that they hadn't caught me. And I think there is a good chance, if they had, that they would have killed me.

Shortly afterwards, I left Highbury Grove School. In five years, it had killed my innocence and turned a big-hearted, enthusiastic little boy into a wary, angry youth. I still can't think of one thing I learned in that school except how to fight.

Just before we left, we all had appointments with the careers teacher. When it came my turn to go in, the guy just stared at me from behind his desk and laughed. 'Well, *you're* going to amount to nothing, Blades!' he smirked. 'It's not even worth talking to you!'

It made it a very short meeting. I could have sworn at the guy but I didn't want to get sent off to the head to get caned one last time. And, in any case, I thought he was probably right.

We L-stream kids didn't sit many exams and the handful that I did were totally futile. I couldn't even read the questions – the letters on the paper just danced and squirmed before my eyes, as ever. And as I couldn't read, I *certainly* couldn't write. I hardly took the top off my pen.

A few weeks later, a mate told me everyone was heading back to school to get their grades, so I went along. There was a list on the wall next to my old classroom, and there was my name on the left-hand side: JASON BLADES.

I ran my eye along the line of letters next to it: U U U U U U U. *Huh?*

'Sir, what does that mean?' I asked a nearby teacher. He squinted at the wall, and sighed.

'It means unclassified, Blades,' he said. 'You haven't got a grade in anything.'

Fair enough. This news didn't really dishearten me because it was exactly what I had expected. *I was unclassified. There you go.* And I left Highbury Grove School without the first idea as to what I wanted to do with my life.

Well, as it turned out, my life had quite a few ideas as to what it wanted to do with me.

3

The great dressing-gown showdown

When I left secondary school, aged sixteen, in the summer of 1986, I immediately fulfilled my career teacher's prediction of my life's trajectory by doing the same thing as the vast majority of my fellow L-stream graduates. I signed on the dole.

Oh yeah, and I also moved in to live with my girlfriend.

This was an extremely young age to begin co-habiting but it seemed to make sense at the time. Maria lived in a block of flats on the far side of Stoke Newington. Her mum had some stuff going on and had absented herself for a little while, so I decided it made sense for me to move in.

My mum knew and liked Maria so she didn't object to me doing it. I am pretty sure she assumed that Maria's mum was also there, looking after us, and I was happy to let Mum think that. I never told her that Maria's mum was away . . . but, then again, she never actually asked me!

Was I ready to live with a girlfriend? I'd have to say no! I was pretty angry and messed up by the racism I was having to endure and the fights I was getting into, plus I still had a very active roving eye for attractive women. Settling down really *wasn't* on my agenda.

So, Maria and I had our ups and downs from the start. When we were getting on well, I'd stay with her. If we'd had a big row, I'd vanish back to Mum's for a few days, and lie and stew in my bed underneath the big mural that said 'JAY' and 'MARIA' and 'LOVE FOREVER'.

Maria was also signing on the rock and roll, so we were only just about scratching by. I soon got bored of that. Whatever my careers teacher thought, I've never liked sitting around doing nothing, and I wanted to get out there and start earning some money so that I could do stuff.

Maria had an African friend called Hassan who always seemed to have a bit of dosh, and once or twice I clocked him heading off the estate early in the morning. The next time I bumped into him, I collared him.

'Where are you going in the mornings?' I demanded.

'I go to get jobs,' he said. 'To get work. Come with me tomorrow if you want and I'll show you.'

The next morning at half past five, Hassan and I set off to walk a couple of miles through Hackney to Cambridge Heath Road. Hassan explained on the way that men looking for casual labour would congregate on a certain street corner, where a gangmaster would dish out cash-in-hand work.

We got there to find a load of mainly African and East European blokes milling around. For thirty minutes, a steady stream of dirty Transit vans pulled up and the burly guy in charge issued orders: 'Right: you, you and you! Get in that van!' He gave Hassan a job. I didn't get one.

This routine of me traipsing through Hackney at sunrise only to trudge back empty-handed went on for a week or so, until one morning a van pulled up and the gangmaster nodded at me: 'You! Go with him!' I climbed in eagerly . . . and got driven two miles to a sausage factory.

It was production-line work. You sat by the conveyer belt with a stack of little cardboard boxes as thousands of frozen long sausages, like you get in hot dogs, rolled down the line towards you. You filled each box with fifty bangers, then went on to the next box.

God, it was boring!

Because the sausages were frozen, in no time your hands were as cold as ice. I was working next to a seventy-year-old white East End lady called Rita. She had a hunchback, as if she had worked there for so long that her body had shaped itself over the production line.

Rita was always cracking a joke, and she was doing her best, but she was struggling to keep up. I'd been there about a week when she held her arthritic, wrinkled fingers out to me. 'Look at me 'ands, Jay!' she said. 'They're freezing! This work ain't good for me!'

I felt sorry for Rita so I started surreptitiously helping to fill up her boxes as well as my own. This soon came to the attention of the supervisor, an obnoxious bloke who would swagger up and down the line, barking orders at us all to work faster.

'How many boxes you done, Rita?' he would ask, then tut and shake his head. 'That's not good enough! You've got to pull your finger out or I'm giving you the tin tack!'

I hated the disrespectful way he was talking to this poor old lady and I decided to have a word. 'You need to leave her alone, mate!' I advised him. He looked surprised, walked up to me and sneered in my face.

'And *you* need to shut your mouth!' he said. 'You're lucky to be working here. Another word from you and you *won't* be!'

Oh, so that was how it was, was it? I bit my tongue. *For now*.

The next day, I was helping Rita out with her boxes when the little Hitler marched along and started giving her a hard time again. He was a bully, and I had learned in the Highbury Grove playground not to tolerate bullies.

'I've told you – shut up and let Rita be!' I told him. 'If I help her, she'll do her quota. Leave her alone!'

The guy did not like being challenged again. He flounced over to me. 'And I've told *you* . . .' he began. He got no further than that, because I smashed him in the face and knocked him clean out.

This foreman was not a popular geezer, and cheers and clapping rang out up and down the conveyor belt. 'Rita, you've got to get out of this place, love,' I told her, as I headed for the door. I didn't stick around to finish my shift. I didn't imagine I'd get paid for it, somehow.

Now, I've never been afraid of hard work and I didn't think that the production-line job was beneath me. Thousands of people do that sort of work every day, and I applaud and admire them for it. But I think I've learned in life that I am quite a creative person – and now, I got the urge to do something a lot more creative.

I got the urge to put on a fashion show.

Spoony and I came up with the idea – I'm not sure exactly where from! I still had the love of clothes that Lloyd had inculcated in me, but if I am honest, I think our main motivation was that it would be a good way for us to meet hot girls.

We blagged the whole thing from start to finish. Spoony and I put the word out on the street that we were after models for a fashion show, and soon we had beautiful girls from Hackney, Islington, Holloway and Archway coming up to us and asking to be involved. *Result!*

We talked a Dalston pub called The Victoria into letting us use their upstairs room, and Spoony and I 'auditioned' the models like two pint-size Simon Cowells of our day. Twenty fit girls promenaded up and down and tried to impress us. We were in teenage-boy heaven!

After we had selected our models, we needed something for them to wear. We went to Hyper Hyper clothes market in High Street Kensington and sweet-talked a couple of stallholders. *We were putting on a big show in east London: could they lend us some gear?*

Amazingly, they loaned us a few armfuls of stuff without even asking for a receipt. We just promised to take it back the day after the show (which we did). A shoe shop in Hackney did exactly the same. *Now* we were in business.

We put posters up to advertise the Saturday-night fashion show and we pulled a decent little crowd. My mum came along to see it. But the evening had a nasty downside.

If I thought that the violence which marred my life would vanish now that I had left school, I was mistaken. My Holly Street Estate nemeses had got wind of what I was up to and, as I proudly escorted the models down the street before the show, a gang of thugs were lying in wait.

Ten lads circled me and began throwing punches. I was ducking and hitting back but then they got me on the floor and got a few kicks in. I managed to escape, but I picked up a couple of bruises and it was not a nice start to the evening.

The girls enjoyed strutting around in the fancy clothes and the show was good but, at the end, I looked out of the pub window to see Holly Street waiting outside for me. I noticed one of them had an axe. The landlord had to call the police to get us out of there safely.

At least they didn't send Blackbeard.

I was casting around for anything I might like to do with my life. I was still signing on, and the unemployment people sent me on a Youth Training Scheme (YTS) course in painting and decorating. A very boring week in a Hackney workshop quickly convinced me that *that* wasn't the career for me.

I was still doing my crack-of-dawn walks through Hackney to pick up casual labouring work. The gangmaster didn't seem to have heard about me decking the sausage-factory foreman, or else he didn't care, because he sent me off to work in a Calor Gas factory.

This was *serious* hard labour! The job entailed putting those hefty Calor Gas bottles into a cage that a guy driving a fork-lift truck would then load onto a lorry. And the bottles weighed an absolute bloody ton.

They came in three different sizes. The smallest ones were just about liftable. The medium-size ones made me feel as if my back would snap in half. I found it impossible to lift the biggest ones: I had to tilt and roll them, being careful not to drop them on my leg and break it.

I was still matchstick-thin at sixteen but most of the blokes working in that factory looked like bodybuilders. I could see why. My three weeks there felt like intensive gym workouts – or prison-camp hard labour! But I have always been a grafter, so I just got on with it.

After that, I got sent off to work in the store room at a Top Shop in the West End. My job was to pick up orders for clothes that were needed on the shop floor, find them in the warehouse and take them up to the assistants on a metal rail.

I was working with a lad called Ebenezer, a young African Cockney piss-taker. We thought it was hilarious to get a request for twenty or thirty garments, and then take the lift to the shop with the rail with just one item of clothing hanging off it. The shop-floor staff didn't seem to find it so hysterical. I lasted three days before I got the sack.

A lot of the labouring work I was being handed at six a.m. was on local building sites. These were an interesting experience as they brought me into contact with a whole new strain of casual racism.

Most of the site labourers were middle-aged East End white blokes with very entrenched attitudes. Their racism wasn't the personal, name-calling stuff I 'd endured in the school playground. It wasn't intended to hurt. They were just channelling the jokes they heard on the telly.

On a hot day they'd tell me, 'It doesn't bother *your lot*, does it? You're used to it!' (They clearly knew nothing about my heatstroke!). If I said I was going to the swimming pool after work, I'd get: 'What for? You coloured blokes can't swim!' It was banter with an edge, a semi-friendly wind-up – and it worked. It wound me up.

I could live with doing the building sites in the summer but when winter rolled around, I knocked them on the head. I was fed up of falling out of bed at five in the morning and walking two miles through pissing rain only to be told by the gangmaster that he had nothing for me that day.

'Come back tomorrow!' he'd say. *No thanks*! I'd think as I trudged disconsolately back home.

I started looking for work through the dole instead. They told me there was a job going as an office junior. I didn't have the slightest idea what one of those was, and I'd never been in an office in my life, but I told them I was up for it.

The job was in New Bond Street in the West End. I found the address and wandered in an open door and up a narrow flight of stairs. It was a hive of activity – people were running up and down the steps looking very busy, and I had to keep squeezing against the wall to let them go by.

I liked the buzz of the place straight away but I had no idea what was going on there. I turned a corner and came to a reception desk, where a woman sat and stared at me. I think I probably looked very out of place.

'Can I help you?' she asked.

'I've come for the job,' I said. 'You know, for the office . . . junior?'

She nodded, and a few minutes later showed me into a big office. A very smart, power-dressed, glamorous middle-aged lady was waiting to interview me.

'Have you got any office experience?' she asked me as I sat down.

'None at all,' I grinned. 'What is it that you do here, then?'

'Oh! You don't know anything about us?'

'Nah! Not a thing!'

'We're a modelling agency,' the woman told me. I smiled at her, and nodded as if she and I belonged on exactly the same level. 'Oh, cool! *I* just organized a fashion show!'

Oddly enough, the interviewer seemed to like the fact that I was totally clueless about what her company were and what they did. We chatted for a bit and she announced that I had got the job. *Start on Monday!*

This felt like good news but it also gave me a problem. I was skint at the time and had no money to get the bus or train from Stoke Newington to the West End every day. I told Spoony this, and he offered to sell me his pushbike for £100. I didn't have it, but I gave him the £30 that I did have, and promised him the rest when I got paid.

Come to think of it, I never got around to paying him that back. I must do it, one day . . .

I loved the model agency job. It was really interesting. The models all had their own cards, with their photos, details and (in those days!) vital statistics on, like 36-24-36. This was years before email, so the agency used to courier these cards by bike to clients who might want to book the models.

My job was to make sure that we had enough cards for all the models and enough photos to go on the cards. This meant that I had to liaise closely with Jan, a Yugoslav photographer with a studio on the top floor of the building.

Every day, I was running up the stairs to Jan's studio for more photos. I would knock on his door and have to wait for a minute because Jan was developing pictures in the dark. I would hear him scrabbling about and putting the light on before I went in.

'What are you doing, then?' I asked him one day. 'Can I have a look?'

Jan let me watch a couple of photo sessions then showed me in detail how he developed the pictures. It was my first introduction to any kind of creativity and it blew me away. I couldn't believe he could make these already attractive women look even more beautiful.

I was so into what he was doing that Jan took a shine to me and gave me a spare old Pentax 100 camera. I took a few pictures of the models myself – not in the sessions, but when they were just sitting around the office – and began looking at London with a photographer's eye.

I spent a weekend or two in Old Street Tube station, where the light was great and the exit tunnels looked brilliant in black and white. At Jan's suggestion, I even went off and did a weekend photography course at Goldsmiths College. It was a really cool hobby.

Because I was up in the West End for work, I also started going out in London a lot more. I would go clubbing with Russell Fraser, the friend who had graffitied my bedroom wall, and a guy called Lee Carroll, who I called Joe 90 because he wore big specs like the puppet TV superhero.

We went to the Wag Club, Busby's and the Limelight, and I was blown away by the cool clothes people were wearing. It made me want to dress differently, too. I started wearing old 1930s trousers, a white shirt, braces and a leather jacket with Doc Martens. I loved that outfit!

Sometimes Maria would come Up West to meet me after work, looking absolutely stunning. We would have some great nights out in London painting the town red (well, on a budget).

One night we were up in Soho, got hungry and went to a burger place called Ed's. We didn't even look at the menu: we just assumed it was like McDonalds, and got burgers, chips, milkshakes, Cokes, the works. I have to give it to them: it was proper good nosh.

When we were done, we asked for the bill and our eyes nearly popped out of our heads: *how much?* We had £30 to last us the week and it cleaned us out. We were left with coppers. We were gutted, but also couldn't stop laughing at how dumb we'd been not to check the prices.

So, Maria and I had some pretty good times up in the glamorous West End. At home, back in her flat in N16, things between us were not so good. In fact, they were getting pretty volatile.

I'll come clean: it was my fault. I have to admit that I was *not* a very faithful boyfriend. There were just too many sexy women catching my teenage eye and I was not about to be satisfied with one of them, even if she *was* the most beautiful girl in Stoke Newington!

I liked the ladies, I had the gift of the gab, and I put it to use to cheat a lot. But I was a really *stupid* cheat. I would go off with girls that Maria knew, or who lived right close to us, or who moved in the same social circle as us. I was rubbish at hiding what I was doing.

Maria was smart as well as beautiful, and she would

always find out and kick me out. Sometimes, I would finish with her and go back to live at Mum's so that I could go with a different girl. Then that would end, and I'd crawl back to Maria and hope that she'd take me back.

Yeah, I was quite a catch!

I could walk around freely and let my guard down when I was out and about in the West End, but around the Hackney area I still had to watch my back. I had too many enemies, too many people had grudges to settle, and I'd always fly off the handle at racist comments or insults.

Spoony and other mates would bollock me: 'Jay, you've *got* to knock the violence on the head, man!' I agreed with them – it wasn't making me happy, or doing me any good – but trouble seemed to follow me around. I'd end up fighting even when I didn't want to.

Islington was still dodgy territory for me, but one Saturday night I went to a house party there with two mates, Horace and Gary. The second that we walked into the main party room I clocked a girl that I had seen around the way that I'd been very much wanting to get to know.

She was leaning against a wall and I went straight over and started chatting her up. One of the local guys spotted this and clearly didn't like it, because he followed me across the room, stood close behind me and started jostling me.

I didn't notice initially, because the room was packed and I was focusing on the girl, but I was vaguely aware of somebody banging into me from behind so many times that it must be on purpose. I looked round and gave the guy a couple of hard stares, but he didn't stop. So . . .

BANG!

Almost as a reflex action, I jabbed my elbow up hard behind me and into the guy's face. I heard a crash behind me. I didn't even look around – I just carried on talking to the girl. Whose mouth was now hanging open in horror.

'You . . . you just knocked that guy out!' she gasped.

'He was asking for it!' I said. 'Now, I need to get your phone number?'

Somebody tugged on my sleeve: 'Jay, Jay! Look!' It was Horace, who was pointing behind me. The guy I had hit was staggering groggily to his feet, helped by his pals, who were gathering around us and looking, to say the least, pretty hostile.

'Shit! Jay, how are we going to get out of this?' Horace whispered.

Sometimes, when you are young and headstrong, you do the stupidest things. I turned back to the girl. 'I'll come back later for your number!' I told her. It may have been my imagination, but she suddenly didn't look *quite* so keen on giving it to me.

The guy I had clobbered was now upright, supported by his pals, and I charged at him and rugby-tackled him. As if I was playing British Bulldog on the estate again, I used him as a battering ram and ran full pelt at his line of mates. They parted in front of me and I zoomed through.

'Quick! Let's go!'

Horace, Gary and I tore out of the house and down the road with a load of geezers from the party chasing after us. They soon gave up and we made it back to Stoke Newington in one piece. Even so, I suspected that that might very well not be the end of it.

It wasn't. A couple of nights later, I was in bed at Maria's when there was a frantic knock at the door. *Huh?* I opened the bedroom window and stared down to see Gary, my mate from the party, waving up at me.

Gary had a severe stutter, especially when he was excited, as he was now: 'J-J-J-Jay! You've got to come down! Is-Is-Is-Islington are here! They've come for r-r-revenge!'

Shit! I was naked, so I grabbed whatever clothes were nearest and threw them on. I had a little rounders bat that I kept to hand in case I ever needed it (a few locals even knew me as Batman) so I grabbed that as well and sprinted out of Maria's flat door and down the stairs.

I saw the Islington mob as soon as I emerged from the flats and ran over to confront them: '*Yeah? Yeah? You want some, do you?*' But they weren't making a move to attack me. They were just . . . staring at me.

I heard Gary's voice behind me. 'J-J-J-Jay! W-w-what are you wearing, bruv?'

I glanced down. What I was wearing, over a pair of boxer shorts, was . . . Maria's mum's dressing gown. It was a fetching little number, kind of lacy, see-through chiffon, with fur around the cuffs and the bottom. It was comple-mented by the fact I also had on her fluffy slippers.

'*Pffft!*' The top dog of the Islington crew wasn't angry any more. He was laughing. He put his fists down, shook his head, turned around and walked off, followed by his smirking mates. I believe their thinking went something like this:

This bloke is willing to fight us dressed like that? We're not fighting him – he's a nutter! In fact, 'Nutter' became my local nickname for a while after that escapade. So, there's a tip on how to stop a nasty fight: dress up like a crazed drag queen!

That particular potential outburst of violence got averted by an unintentional bit of slapstick. The next time, I was not so lucky.

I was at my mum's house with Maria and a friend of hers called Karen, getting ready to go for a night out. Karen was dating an older guy from a pretty rough family. He got wind somehow that she was round at my house, didn't like it, and turned up on the doorstep.

Karen went out to talk to him and he started shouting at her. I wasn't sure what to do. The guy was really like an elder to me, and I'd always been taught to respect my elders, but I didn't like the way that he was carrying on to Karen.

I put my head around the door. 'Hey, man, do you mind keeping the noise down a bit, please?' I asked politely. He stared at me and didn't even bother to answer.

I went back indoors but the guy kicked off again. He was cussing and swearing at Karen and sounded like he might turn nasty. I decided to have another word and reappeared on the doorstep.

'Sorry, but can you stop swearing like that?' I asked. 'It's my mum's house and she is upstairs. Please show some respect!'

Karen's boyfriend turned to me, looked me up and down and clicked his teeth. 'Listen, boy, you need to shut your mouth and go and suck out your mummy!' he hissed.

Wow! That guy had just triggered me in so many ways at once! Abusing Karen *and* me, disrespecting my mother, *calling me 'boy'* . . . I was so shocked that I almost staggered backwards. *Shit!*

I turned around and ran up the stairs quickly to find my rounders bat. I bumped into Justin at the top of the stairs.

'Hey, bruv, have you seen my bat?' I asked him.

'Why do you want it?' said Justin.

'That geezer downstairs just told me to go and suck out our mum!'

Justin stared, looked as horrified as me, and vanished into his room. I found my bat and ran back downstairs. By now, the pissed-off boyfriend had gripped Karen by the arms and was shaking her about and roughing her up.

'Let go of her!' I shouted and grabbed Karen from him. At the same moment, I suddenly saw Justin, who had run downstairs and out of the back door of the house, appear behind the geezer. Holding a little hammer.

The guy stepped towards me and clenched his fists. 'Can't you see she's my girl?' he yelled at me. *What the fuck is wrong with you, boy?*

'Boy'! Again! That was it. The red mist descended.

Without even thinking, I swung the rounders bat and smacked him with it on top of his head. The bloke staggered backwards . . . at which point, Justin hit him on the back of his head with the hammer. *Knockout!* Karen's boyfriend slumped to the ground and was out for the count.

Now what do we do? Well, we did have a big night out planned . . .

'Are you ready?' I called to Maria. She, Karen and I stepped right over Karen's unconscious boyfriend and headed off Up West. When we got back, in the early hours of the morning, he had gone. I didn't know where and I didn't really care.

That incident was to have serious repercussions for me.

The boyfriend and Karen were both from proper naughty, heavyweight local families and neither of them were impressed with what had gone down. I got a terrifying message via a mate a few days later.

I had disrespected an elder and I had to pay. They were going to kill me!

It sounds crazy, but I knew both of these families and I knew that they wouldn't say that without meaning it. *Jesus! Now what do I do?* As it happened, we had a cousin who was a local elder, and Justin spoke to him and got him to negotiate with the angry families on my behalf.

They had a meeting, and they reached an agreement. OK, they would spare me serious bad punishment for what I had done. But I had to go away. *I had to get out of Stoke Newington.*

It sounds tough but it was actually a relief. *I would take that.* It was better than getting a severe beating, or worse – and, in any case, Stoke Newington didn't feel a safe place for me to be right now. Maria and I moved in with her Uncle Lawrence and his partner, Sharon, two miles away in Clapton.

It was a hard time. I had quit my modelling agency job – they had got rid of my mate Jan, the photographer, and I didn't like it there so much without him. It meant that I was back on the dole again and hanging around the house all day long.

It was nice of Maria's uncle to help us out and take us in but it wasn't working out. Now I wasn't working, it felt claustrophobic. I didn't like not being able to go to see my mum safely, and Maria and I weren't getting on again, for all of the usual reasons.

I had been secretly seeing a girl called Rachel on the side. Maria found out, as she always did, and she got the proper hump this time. She kicked me out of her uncle's house. I couldn't blame her, but it meant I had to find somewhere new to live sharpish.

When it comes to accommodation the dole doesn't stretch far, but a friend helped me out. I bumped into an old mate from school called Joe, who knew of a room going on a council estate behind the Sadler's Wells ballet theatre in Clerkenwell, just down the road from Islington.

I went to see it. It was a mouldy old bedsit: a bare room with a mattress on the floor, a chair, a kettle and not a lot else. But beggars can't be choosers, so I moved into that grotty dump and sat on my solitary chair feeling spectacularly sorry for myself.

I had just turned eighteen – how had I ended up here? I looked hard at my situation and I could see how, in a way, it was my fault that I had got into this predicament. But, at the same time, it also felt unfair, as if life was dealing me a spectacularly shit hand.

Joe also had some work to offer me. He had turned into a bit of an entrepreneur since school and opened up a little shop on the Angel in Islington, selling second-hand women's clothing. He also had a stall on Camden Market at weekends doing the same thing.

I started helping him out. Joe would send me up to a wholesale clothes place in Old Street with some money to buy boxes of 1920s and 1930s women's silk dresses. They were stupidly cheap, and Joe could put a big mark-up on the stuff when he sold it in the shop.

I quite enjoyed working in the shop and I didn't need

to turn on the spiel to the customers too much because the dresses were so nice that they were flying off the shelves. They sold themselves. They were sexy and figure-hugging – I could have put one on myself and looked good.

Well, maybe not!

I also spent some time on the stall at Camden. We could make decent money there. One time, Joe came in pleased because he had got hold of a load of Katherine Hamnett blouses and silk shirts. Oddly enough, they didn't sell all that well.

The clothes job was fun and it bailed me out for a few weeks, but it still felt temporary and short term. I was killing time, really, so I was pretty receptive when my mum came to Clerkenwell to visit me with a radical suggestion for a major change in our living situation.

Mum could see that I was low and she hated that I couldn't live with her and Justin because of the grief I had got into in Stoke Newington. She wanted to get the family back together again, and she thought the best way to do it was for us to get out of London.

Auntie Jackie and Uncle Tim had recently moved up to Luton with my cousins, and Mum said Auntie Jackie had been on the phone every day, telling her that it was really cheap compared to London, it was an OK place to live, and we should follow them. Mum had been convinced and had put a deposit down to buy an ex-council house up there.

What did I think? Basically, I figured: *Yeah, why not?*

I had lived in London for all of my life, and it was all that I knew, but it wasn't working out for me right now. I had no direction to my life, no masterplan, and, looking around my crappy bedsit, I didn't exactly have a lot to lose. *Yes!* I thought. *A fresh start is exactly what I need!*

So, that was settled. We were all going to go and live in Luton.

4

The sins of my father

I WENT TO LUTON AHEAD OF THE REST OF MY FAMILY. My mum had already put a deposit down on a house and it was ready for us to move in, but she had to work her notice at her job in London. She also wanted Justin to have a chance to finish secondary school.

It made sense for me to get out of London as soon as possible so, aged eighteen, I moved up to Luton on my own to wait for them and start setting up our new home. I've always liked fresh starts and it felt, if anything, like an exciting opportunity. *OK, here we go! A new life!*

The house was on quite a rough estate in an area called Bury Park. It was nice that Uncle Tim and Auntie Jackie were already up there with my cousins so I wasn't totally alone as I settled in. But I soon began to recognize something a bit familiar about my new life.

It seemed very like my old life.

I wanted to earn money but, as ever, I was handicapped by the fact that I couldn't read or write. *How do you apply for a job if you can't even read the details on the card, let alone fill in the application form?* So, I stuck with what I knew: casual labouring.

The good thing about building-site work is you can just turn up on a site and ask if you can have a go. If you work hard, the foreman will ask you to go back the next day, and the day after that, or guarantee you a month's cash-in-hand work.

As I said, I've never been afraid of hard graft, so I knuckled down and got building houses. Through one of the sites, I met a lovely Irish geezer called Peter O'Toole. He wasn't a film star, he was a property mogul, and he soon had a steady stream of work going for me.

So that was one similarity to my life in Stoke Newington. Another was racism – and fighting.

I found a racist undertone to life in Luton that was different from what I was used to in London. Quite a lot of working-class white blokes – and a lot of them were football fans – made it clear that they didn't like either black people or the town's very sizeable Asian community.

Right from day one, if I went out in Luton with Tom or Leroy or any of my cousins, I knew at some point we'd be likely to hear taunting insults: 'Oi, you black bastards!' And, just the same as in London, just the same as with Iqbal's glasses, I wouldn't back down or run away.

I might have moved thirty miles to the sticks but I was still the same easily-wound-up teen. *If they wanted trouble, I'd give it to them.*

And, almost before I knew it, I'd got myself a bit of a local reputation. *Here we go again!*

I got friendly with a few Asian guys on the Bury Park Estate who offered me another way to make money. They controlled a lot of the local dope-dealing trade, and they asked me if I'd be interested in doing a few deliveries for them.

Sure, why not? I didn't touch the stuff myself, after my bad experience with the youth-club supervisor, but I knew how the game worked from seeing the frontline in Dalston. So, I started doing a few drop-offs and earning a little cash to top up my building-site money.

After I'd been in Luton for six months or so, Mum and Justin moved up to join me. It was great to see them, but I found it hard to get used to living in Mum's disciplined household again. I had enjoyed the freedom of living on my own – and once you've left home, it's hard to go back.

Plus, I was missing Maria.

When we had finished after she caught me cheating on her yet again in London, I had sort of lost touch with Maria. But she had some family in America, and I had heard on the grapevine that she was spending time with them there and having an extended holiday.

I managed to get a number for her and phoned her up. I told her that I missed her, and that I had moved to Luton and was trying to make a new life for myself. Would she like to try again?

She said that she would.

Result! I was made up. I was earning enough to rent us a flat on another nearby housing estate, Marsh Farm, and was waiting for Maria there by the time that she flew back from the States two weeks later. She moved in with me and we picked up exactly where we had left off in Stoke Newington.

Except for one major difference. Within a few weeks, she was pregnant.

You wouldn't exactly call it planned. Maria and I weren't trying to have a baby, but I suppose, thinking about it, we weren't making any great efforts *not* to have one, either. The news came out of the blue – and yet, when Maria told me, I was over the moon.

I still wasn't quite out of my teens and yet, in a funny way, it felt the right time for me to become a dad. *OK!* I thought. *Things are going to change around here!* I imagined having a kid would bring a new focus to my life and help me to sort myself out.

I wanted a child to give me responsibility and lend my life a purpose that it lacked. My existence was kind of aimless but *this would make everything alright!* I did 0–60 in ten seconds: I'd never thought about it before but, suddenly, I had a burning desire to be a dad.

I suppose I thought that it would make me a better person.

Maria and I mostly got on OK through the pregnancy, knowing we had this huge thing ahead of us. Mum was delighted and helped us to buy a few baby bits and bobs and, on 4 October 1990, Maria and I went off to Luton and Dunstable Hospital. *This was it!*

Some men say watching their child being born is a very emotional and moving experience but, if I'm honest, I didn't find that. I wanted to be there and I knew Maria needed my support, but my main impression of childbirth was how much hard work it is – and how graphic!

I have a pretty high pain threshold but, as I watched Maria give birth, my main thought was, *I am glad I am not a woman – because that looks a grim thing to go through!* I was seeing things I just wasn't ready to see. *Too much information!*

It was grisly, but I'm glad I was there because it made me appreciate the pain women have to go through in childbirth. I'm amazed that any woman ever has more than one child. Any bloke would be like: *'Go through THAT again? No, thank you!'*

Thankfully, nothing lasts forever. 'It's a boy!' said the midwife, as the sound of crying filled the room. It was cool to hold my son, and to see Maria cradling him, and I felt as proud as any dad as we took him back to Marsh Farm.

We called him Levi. It was mostly Maria's choosing, but I was happy with it because I wanted him to have a short name. I just can't be arsed with long names – maybe that's why I shortened mine from Jason to Jay!

Then I got down to the routine of being a father.

The emotional connection to Levi that I hadn't felt at his birth soon came. I was laying him in his cot one night and put my little finger in his tiny hand. Levi squeezed it. *Wow!* I felt a glow, and a jolt of electricity like in that Michelangelo painting of lightning connecting two hands at the start of *The South Bank Show*. It was amazing – so moving!

I got the hang of some parenting jobs quickly. I got adept at changing nappies, feeding him and knowing when he needed to sleep. Levi had bad colic, so I took him for a lot of long walks in his pram or papoose to try to stop him crying and calm him down.

Yet, at twenty, fatherhood didn't come easy to me. It felt weird – *and why wouldn't it?* I was trying to be a father while having never seen anyone fulfil that role first-hand before. I had no experience of being a dad . . . *because I'd never had one.*

You don't get a manual when you become a dad. It's like someone throws you a ball and says, 'Go and play football!' when you've never seen the game before. What do you do: pick up the ball? Throw it over your head? *Sit on it?* You're guessing. You haven't got a clue.

I was still working the building sites so Maria would look after Levi all day. When I got in at teatime, she'd be at her wits' end from his crying and go to her friend's house for a break. My evenings became a long, repetitive ritual of howling, burping and Calpol.

I couldn't complain, it was what having a baby was about – but it felt alien. I had hoped that when I became a dad, it would make me more responsible and help me understand my role in society better. I'd hoped it would fill my emptiness; fill the hole in my soul.

But it just wasn't happening. I felt the same as ever.

I spent a year trying to be the normal-dad guy who comes home from work and puts his money on the table. A year feeding and cuddling Levi and pushing him around Luton in his buggy. But the routine was getting to us, and Maria and I had started arguing again. Badly.

I had thought that I was ready to be a dad – but I really, really wasn't.

I wanted to stick it out and make it work because, more

than anything, I didn't want to repeat the sins of my father. *I didn't want to be my dad.* I wasn't about to become The Man Who Contributed Towards Levi's Birth. But it all felt wrong. I was confused, angry . . . and I felt trapped.

What to do? More and more, I felt like I wanted out. And, I'm sorry to say, instead of facing up to the problems with Maria, I started getting distracted by someone else. I guess it was my way of finding an escape route.

My cousin Leroy's girlfriend had a friend in London called Romany, who came up to visit. As soon as I saw Romany, my eyes were on stalks. She was so pretty, and I reacted exactly as I always did to pretty girls back then: *Damn, you're beautiful! I want you!* She seemed interested in me, too.

Maybe becoming a father should turn off your roving eye and make you naturally become faithful to your partner – well, perhaps it works like that for some blokes, but it *certainly* didn't for me. Meeting Romany helped to make the decision for me.

I told Maria that I was leaving and moving back to London.

It was a painful conversation – she and I certainly had plenty of experience of splitting up, but not in this situation. Not with a kid. And yet it's a sign of how young I still was, and how immature, that I still knew that I was definitely going to do it.

I moved back to Mum's for a few days while I prepared to return to London. Mum was really upset that I was going, and leaving Maria and Levi . . . and it led her to introduce me to somebody that I *really* wasn't expecting to meet.

Justin was as hot-headed as me and he hadn't left his propensity for getting in trouble behind when we moved to Luton. He got into a big fight and ended up hospitalized. It upset the hell out of me – *Shit! Nobody does that to my baby brother!*

I got my cousins and a few other mates together. We were standing on a street corner, trying to decide whether to go to see Justin in hospital or to pay his attackers a little visit, when, out of the corner of my eye, I saw Mum walking towards me.

Huh? What's she doing here? She never comes around this part of town!

Mum wasn't alone. Uncle Tim was with her, and there was a guy that I didn't recognize – an unremarkable-looking black guy. *Who was that?* The question was answered as soon as Mum walked up to me.

'Jason,' she said. 'This is your father.'

What the . . .? It totally threw me. It was the last thing I expected. I think my mouth actually fell open as I looked the geezer up and down.

This was him? The Man Who Contributed Towards My Birth? The geezer I last saw when I was five years old, and hadn't set eyes on for fifteen years since?

How did I feel?

The truth is that I felt . . . *nothing*. No excitement, no anger . . . *nothing*. I wasn't one of those abandoned kids who always wondered what their dad was like. Mine had made it clear for years, by his absence, how unimportant I was in his life. And I felt precisely the same way about him.

What's he doing here? I wondered, angrily. *Why's he come? Why now?*

'Mum, I haven't got time for this!' I told her. 'I've got something to do. Then I'm going to see Justin in hospital.'

Mum gave me a look. 'Jason! This is your father!' she admonished me. 'Speak to him!'

TMWCTMB and I mumbled a few words to each other. He didn't seem any more excited to see me than I was to see him. But we arranged to meet up again later, when I had finished my business in hand.

When I met him again that evening, I took him to see Maria and Levi. *To see his grandson.* When we walked into the front room, Levi was in his high chair, and he stared at me, then at the other geezer, then back at me. I saw the thought bubble over his tiny head: *Huh?*

Little kids can't hide their feelings, and I could see Levi puzzling: *That's my dad, but who's that other guy, who looks like him?* I didn't detect many facial similarities between me and TMWCTMB – because I didn't want to. Maria said later that we looked a lot like each other.

TMWCTMB and I sat and tried to talk but it was awkward and we didn't connect. He looked like he had no more idea why he was there than I did, and it was a relief for both of us when he said he had to go. But we agreed to meet up again in London.

Mum never asked me how the encounter had gone, but it had clearly been her idea. Years later, she told me she'd been upset I was leaving Maria and Levi, feared it was history repeating itself – *have a child, then run away* – and wanted my father to try to talk me out of it.

Mum had meant well. But there was *nobody* I was less likely to listen to, or take moral guidance from, than TMWCTMB.

I left Luton. Romany was living with her cousin in south London and I moved in with them. The house was crowded and, after a few days, Romany said she had an uncle who was going to China for a while and we could stay in his empty house in Lewisham.

Once we got there, we didn't last long. We just didn't have much in common. I didn't feel as guilty as I should have about leaving Maria and Levi, but it felt weird to go from my long-term partner and my baby son to living with a girl who, really, I hardly knew.

I was antsy, twitchy and probably a nightmare to be around and it was no big surprise when Romany told me to leave. So, I did. The only problem was that I had nowhere to go.

I didn't want to trail back to Luton with my tail between my legs, and it didn't seem a good idea to show my face in Stoke Newington again yet. I was effectively a homeless person. So, I went to a homeless hostel.

The Salvation Army took me in at a place they ran in Elephant and Castle. I basically had a bed in a dorm and that was it. They were mostly older blokes in there, and I heard some very weird, disturbing noises at night. *Wow, some people can really cough!*

I had just turned twenty-one and this was not a good way to celebrate . . . yet, in a strange way, I took it in my stride. *I started life in a homeless hostel,* I thought to myself. *And here I am again!* I guess, like they say, sometimes you have to laugh or else you'd cry.

It was winter, there was no building-site work, and I didn't have a lot to do during the days. I remember sitting in the hostel's TV room watching daytime telly, which really *isn't* me. So, for want of anything better to do, I went to see my dad again.

The Man Who Contributed Towards My Birth was living in a council house in Stonebridge, northwest London, with his partner. He opened the door, walked me through his front room and nodded towards three teenagers who were sitting there.

'See over there, right? That's your brothers and sister!' he muttered, brusquely.

What the . . .? I was shocked. This seemed a rather off-hand introduction for such potentially major characters in my life! TMWCTMB didn't say any more than that, so I took it upon myself to go over and say hello to – apparently – my new siblings.

The girl was called Sandra and was a couple of years younger than me and the boys were Lucas and Lewis and were in their early teens. They were all friendly, but as we got to chatting, TMWCTMB called me over.

'Come in here!' he said. We went into the kitchen and sat down. I had a burning opening question for him.

'I've got other brothers and sisters, right?' I asked. 'I remember coming to your house when I was little, and there was Samantha and Kara . . .'

TMWCTMB interrupted me brusquely. 'No, no!' he said. He pointed back at the sitting room. '*This* is all my children. That's all you've got.'

'But . . .'

'I told you no! There's nobody else!'

'Oh. OK.'

We tried to talk, but it went no better than in Luton. TMWCTMB was more confident in how he spoke to me now he was on his home turf. It was clear he was an old-fashioned, macho Jamaican man with very definite views on how our relationship should work.

He saw it this way: I was his child. He was my elder. I had to respect him. I wasn't to challenge him or ask him anything.

Well, as I saw it, the only problem with *that* was that respect has to be earned – and he had never done a thing in my life to deserve it.

Not a single thing.

TMWCTMB explained a little bit about himself. He was a carpenter who also did some occasional work as an architect. He was involved in a local community centre, Bridge Park, but, basically, he was a chippy who did building-site work.

He told me this, but he didn't ask me any questions about me. Then he abruptly stood up: 'C'mon, we're going!' He didn't say where to. As we left, I said goodbye to my new sister, Sandra, and swapped phone numbers.

TMWCTMB walked me around the corner to another house, where there were three older people waiting. 'This is my mum, and my brother and my sister!' he said. As I was shaking hands, he walked out and left me with them.

This was getting to be quite the headfuck! A seriously weird day! I sat and chatted to them. They were nice. His sister told me how my dad had been very hurt as a boy when his mum left him in Jamaica. She said he had been trying to *prove himself as a man* in London ever since.

I listened to her words . . . but they didn't mean a lot to me. I didn't feel sorry for TMWCTMB, or sympathetic towards him. I felt the same as I had always felt towards him: *nothing*. I didn't hate him. I felt emotionless. Indifferent.

But I knew that I didn't trust him.

Back in the Salvation Army hostel, a guy called Michael Arlington came to see me. He was a middle-aged white man who was a trustee of the hostel and very involved with the Church of England. Michael was also, by a million miles, the poshest person I'd ever met in my life.

He seemed a lovely geezer and talked as if he wanted to help me, which threw me. It made me suspicious. I wasn't used to anyone like him taking the slightest interest in people like me: *What did he want?* But Michael had what sounded a decent proposition.

He asked if I would like to move out of the hostel and into a halfway-house flat that I would share with other young homeless people. I was keen to get away from the night-time coughing and spluttering in the dorm, and it sounded like progress, so I agreed.

Michael moved me and three other young guys into a council flat on the Peabody Estate in Bethnal Green, back in the East End. I didn't know them and we were all from different parts of the country – I remember one came from Liverpool. We were wary of each other.

I still had no work and it was an aimless time living in that flat. I did a couple of trips up to Luton to see Levi – and I called up my new sister, Sandra, to chat. At which point, she unleashed a complete bombshell.

I knew that I didn't trust The Man Who Contributed Towards My Birth and now I realized how right I was. Sandra told me the truth. When TMWCTMB had said I only had three siblings via him, he had been talking bullshit. The Man Who Contributed Towards My Birth had also been contributing towards many, many more.

I had a whole load more half-brothers and half-sisters than three. In fact, Sandra said, *I had twenty-five.*

Fucking! Hell! I couldn't believe my ears. *Twenty-five?!* Yet it showed my instincts were spot on when it came to TMWCTMB. He and I had sat down to talk. I had asked him a major question about my life, and my family. He had looked me in the eye . . . and lied to me.

It was overwhelming to get my head around, but I knew I wanted to meet this mystery army of unknown siblings. I wanted to track them down. Sandra said she could help me. But, for now, I had something else on my mind.

I had come to realize Michael Arlington didn't have a hidden agenda – he was just a kind-hearted guy who wanted to give struggling young people a leg-up in life. He suggested that I go to see an agency in King's Cross called the Community Voluntary Service, or CVS.

I had bugger-all else to do, so I went up and had a chat with a couple of nice, earnest people. Michael gave me a reference that was probably far more generous than I deserved: I don't know, I couldn't read it! The CVS guys asked me about myself, then made me an offer.

They said I could go to Oxford to work at a Christian-run charity and homeless hostel called the Cyrenians. I would be a volunteer but they'd give me a little bit of money, and a roof over my head, and feed me. So, what did I think?

My reaction was basically the same as when Mum had suggested moving to Luton, two years earlier: *Sure, why not? I've got nothing going on here!* I have always been a glass-half-full sort of bloke. OK, Luton hadn't worked out, but . . . *who knows? Could Oxford give my life the kickstart it needed?*

Well, there was only one way to find out.

5

A Niagara Falls of lurid orange treacle

I WAS LOOKING FORWARD TO MOVING TO OXFORD BUT my arrival there was not auspicious. I got off the bus from London in the picturesque city centre and had a butcher's at a place I'd never been to in my life before. All around me, as far as the eye could see, all I could see was white people.

Wow! I had never seen so many uninterrupted white faces before! There was not a black guy to be seen! I think I might have had a bit of a panic attack on the spot, because I called my mum up.

'Mum, there are no other black people here!' I told her. 'I think I've made a big mistake!'

'Don't worry about it, Jason!' Mum said. 'You'll be fine!' I was grateful for the reassurance, but not entirely sure that I agreed with her.

I made my way to the Cyrenians homeless centre and

got introduced to Sandra, a really welcoming black lady who was their rehousing officer. Then I saw another black woman, and a black guy. I relaxed internally and let my guard down slightly: *OK, maybe this might work, after all!*

Sandra was to become quite influential on my life. She was a very cool Rasta woman who became like a big sister to me. She was very clued in and politically engaged, and over the next few months she opened my eyes to a lot of injustice in society. For now, I was still pretty naïve.

I had agreed to be a volunteer but, if I am honest, I didn't have the first idea what volunteering was, or what to expect at the Cyrenians. I knew it was a homeless centre: *well, so what?* I had been to a few of them before: in fact, I was technically homeless myself, at the moment!

But this place was something else again. It was a complete eye-opener and it blew my mind.

This was a major step down from any homeless centre I had ever seen before. It was a hostel full of people – mostly older men – who had absolutely nothing: people who had given up on society, on family, on hygiene, basically on *life*. They had absolutely fuck-all in the world.

I had thought *I* had been doing badly and my life had been going wrong. Well, walking into Cyrenians instantly gave me a whole new perspective. Compared to *these* poor guys, I was a king.

The people who ran the centre sorted me out with a room nearby and explained what my job as a volunteer would entail. It was pretty basic stuff. I would make sandwiches and cups of tea and dish them out, run errands, give out the residents' tablets and, most importantly, sit down with them and talk to them. Be company. Get to know them.

My other jobs involved washing the clothes the residents arrived in, which, if I am honest, could be a bit stomach-turning . . . and delousing them.

Old geezers arrived at the Cyrenians in a hideous condition. Their backs would be covered in shit, because they were homeless and had reached the point where they wouldn't even bother to pull down their trousers and pants and shit behind a bush. They would just crap themselves.

I was told to greet the men when they arrived, take them to the bathroom, tell them to strip off and drench them with the shower hose. Basically, I had to hose them down. I needed to wash them, shave their heads and put their clothes in a bag to throw them away – or, in the worst cases, burn them.

There were a lot of worst cases! We were lucky that local stores such as The Gap used to donate their unsold shirts, jeans and sweaters for our guys to wear. Because the stuff they were wearing when they arrived really was *not* fit for purpose.

I'll never forget one of the first men I had to delouse. He was a Rasta bloke named Goldie, who had body lice jumping all over him when he stripped off. His waist-length dreadlocks looked like they were held together with dirt, dust and shit. *God knows what was living deep in there!*

Most Rasta guys won't let you even *touch* their dreadlocks, they see them as sacred, but Goldie knew that his were in such a two-and-eight that he didn't even object when I said I'd have to chop them off: 'Yeah, yeah, alright, man!' I took a deep breath. This might be worse than watching Levi being born!

Goldie sat down and I got the clippers and started shaving his head. The first huge dreadlock hit the bathroom floor with a loud CLUNK! as if it was a plank of wood, and hundreds of tiny creatures scuttled out of it and ran in every direction. *Eucch!*

Even Goldie looked shocked. And I quickly began to learn that being squeamish was not a luxury that was open to me at Oxford Cyrenians.

'Culture shock' does not begin to describe it. I had never met people like this; people who had reached the bottom of the barrel and carried on falling. I was amazed at the fact that so many of them had absolutely nothing yet were still able to have a laugh and a joke. Which they were.

In a weird way, those guys were inspirational. From the start, I threw myself into looking after them, feeding them, bathing them, talking to them and befriending them. And I discovered something about myself that absolutely astonished me.

I was really, really good at it.

I had mostly done dead-end jobs before, but now, given the chance to help people in their lives, I found that I had a whole load of compassion. I'd always thought I didn't give a damn about anyone or anything. I had no idea I had this *kindness* in me.

I had always hated injustice, ever since Iqbal's glasses, but the only way I'd ever known to combat it was fighting: to lose my rag and start beating the crap out of people. Suddenly, Oxford Cyrenians was giving me the chance to do something good without violence. It was a revelation.

I surprised myself. I was great at getting on with the old guys in the hostel. Great at communicating with them.

Great at *connecting*. I liked them, and they liked me. *Bloody hell! Who'd have thought it?*

I think I stood out a bit from the other volunteers. They were all white and a lot of them were very middle class, brainy and wealthy. They had just been travelling, to Ethiopia or Cambodia, and their parents were funding their gap year before they went to college or began their careers.

I'm not slagging those guys off. They meant well and their hearts were in the right place. But they didn't come from the streets, or the ghetto, and they'd had no hardships in their lives. When they sat and tried to talk to the residents, they could come over as patronizing.

I wasn't like that. I knew what it was like to come from a disadvantaged background. I knew poverty, and hard times, and violence, and bigotry. And what I was now learning was: *I knew how to talk to people.*

The Cyrenians management could see that I had fitted right in and was doing well because, after I had been at the centre for six months, they asked me to stop being a volunteer and join the staff as a full-time paid care worker. I was delighted. The job was rewarding, and now I was to be rewarded for doing it well.

They gave me a bit of on-the-job training: how to lift heavy residents; how to get the disabled old guys in and out of the bath; how to change a colostomy bag; how to look out for alcoholism and drug abuse. It was all useful and I picked it up quickly.

Most important of all, though, was how to talk to people, how to have a laugh with them, and how to treat them with respect, no matter what their situation and condition. And that was where I was turning out to be a bit of a natural.

I loved the place and I loved the job. There was human tragedy at the Cyrenians, for sure, but there was also comedy. *So* much comedy. I can't even begin to remember just how many times I found myself bent over double and weeping tears of laughter.

Because we had so many alcoholics, and people with mental-health issues, alcohol was banned at the hostel, and anybody who had been drinking was not allowed on the premises. This didn't deter some of our most intrepid residents from trying.

Foremost among them was a guy called Roy. Roy had been a big drinker for years and he wasn't minded to quit. We had to keep an eye on him, and one day I was standing by the front door of the hostel when he came weaving in, looking proper unsteady.

I stopped him: 'Roy, you've been drinking! You can't come in.'

'I haven't!' Roy protested. 'I haven't had a drop.'

'You have, man!' I said. 'You look well wavy.'

'How can I get a drink?' Roy asked. 'You know I'm banned from all the pubs and off-licences!' Which was true.

I was staring at him, puzzled, when Roy 'fessed up with a grin.

'I've been drinking aftershave.'

Ha! So, he had been necking Chateau Old Spice! 'Roy, your farts are gonna smell lovely down at the night shelter tonight!' I said. 'But you can't come in here!'

One geezer who needed a lot of looking after was a guy called Dodi, who was a diabetic who also had no legs. He was about sixty and quite a stocky bloke, and I always found it heavy work to lift him out of his wheelchair when it came time to wash him.

Dodi was normally OK to deal with, but every couple of months or so he would get pissed off with life in the hostel, and announce that he was leaving in very dramatic fashion.

'I've fucking had enough of this place!' he'd yell. 'Fuck this! I'm out of here!'

I'd try to talk him down: 'Come on, Dodi, bruv! It's OK! Calm down!' It would be to no avail.

'Fuck the lot of you!' he would roar. By now, he would be crashing his wheelchair repeatedly into the closed front door. 'Open this door and let me out!'

Cyrenians wasn't a prison. If he wanted to go, we had to let him. Dodi would head off down the street with a couple of other guys in tow. His disabilities meant that he got more money in benefits than anybody else, so they knew he could afford to stand them a drink or two. A day or two would pass, and then Dodi would roll back in as if nothing had happened.

The job was satisfying like nothing I had ever known before and it gave me a sense of purpose that I loved. My life in Oxford felt as if it was working out well – although it was not without its occasional mishaps.

The hostel managers had sorted me a room a couple of miles away from work and I used to catch the bus home after my shifts. One day I had a quick pee after work, in case it was a long wait for the bus, and raced off to the stop.

There were a couple of gay pubs next to the Cyrenians, and as I strode purposefully past them, I noticed the drinkers standing outside looking at me. *Were they checking me out? That didn't usually happen!* But they were staring at me very weirdly.

I also seemed to be getting attention from the people at the bus stop as I walked to the back of the queue. The older black lady in front of me in the line turned around, appearing shocked, looked me in the eye, and then stared down at my fly area. I followed her gaze.

I was walking around with my penis hanging out.

Oh, shit! I had dashed out of the loo without checking myself properly! But I looked so embarrassed as I apologised, and scrambled to pull up my zip, that I think the lady could tell I was just a bit of a berk and not a pervert flasher. I hope so, anyway!

When I wasn't making an exhibition of myself, I was getting settled in Oxford. It felt like I actually had some grounding and direction to my life. I think Maria could see it, as well, and she started bringing Levi over from Luton to see me some weekends.

I also set about the task of trying to track down my secret family.

After she had broken the bombshell news to me that I had twenty-five siblings, I had kept in touch with my sister, Sandra, and we talked a lot on the phone. And she told me a horror story that illustrated just how reckless The Man Who Contributed Towards My Birth was in the way that he scattered his seed far and wide.

Sandra told me that she had fancied a local boy who also seemed to like her. They had done a bit of flirting, and had just got to the point where they seemed likely to kiss and to start seeing each other. However, nothing had ever happened between them – and then her brother, Lucas, told her not to go any further with him.

Sandra thought it was just Lucas being over-protective and trying to shield his sister from predatory boys. She reacted angrily – until he put her straight.

'No, sis, don't you know?' he asked her. 'That guy is another one of our dad's. He's our *brother*, sis!'

Wow. Just wow.

Sandra was in contact with a lot of our half-brothers and -sisters and she helped to put me in touch. They were all living with their various mums in different bits of north-west London, near where TMWCTMB was based, so I made a few weekend trips there.

Sandra introduced me to a sister called Sophia, who is five years younger than me. Sophia is brilliant and she and I struck up a really nice relationship straight away. Shortly after we met, she made a trip up to Oxford to see me.

I also met a cool brother called Michael, who was a similar age to Sophia and was living in Harlesden with his mum and his – and my – younger brother, Neil. They were all happy to meet me. I guess it was cool for them suddenly to have a grown-up elder brother they'd never heard of before!

That made sense to me because the sibling I *really* wanted to know was Samantha – the big sis I had met so briefly when I was five. Ever since Mum had said I was the 'man of the house', I'd always had to be the grown-up one in our family. It made Samantha special in my mind: *Wow, she is older than me!*

My heart went *boom boom boom!* every time I thought about her. But Sandra didn't know Samantha because

Samantha was before her time. And I couldn't ask TMWCTMB about her . . . because he'd already told me that she didn't exist.

Some of my new siblings were teenagers and some weren't even that old yet. Sandra took me to a birthday party in Stonebridge for a little sister, Noma, who was just turning eleven. TMWCTMB turned up for that one.

He and I didn't say a lot to each other, but at one stage I was standing with Sophia when TMWCTMB came over to talk to her. By now he had just split up from Sandra's mum, and he seemed quite keen to broadcast his latest romantic situation.

'I'm seeing a girl now who is only a few years older than you!' he told Sophia.

Man! I thought. *I'm not really sure that's something that you should be boasting about! Not to your daughter!*

Outside of that chance meeting, I didn't have any direct contact with TMWCTMB and nor did I want to. We had no relationship and that was fine by me. In fact, as I met more and more of his kids, what amazed me was how OK some of them seemed with his lifestyle.

I guess they were young – and also, TMWCTMB had been present, or semi-present, in some of their childhoods. He had dipped in and out of their lives every now and then. It just seemed to be from *me* that The Man Who Contributed Towards My Birth had absented himself completely.

Over a few months, Sandra introduced me to eleven of my new brothers and sisters. *Eleven!* I enjoyed meeting them, they were great kids . . . but then I had to stop for a while. Because it was doing my head in.

There were just so many of them! It was a lot to cope

with, time-wise and mentally. Some of them were super-young . . . and, in any case, I had other things going on in my own life.

Life was still rolling along great at the Cyrenians, and things got even better there when I picked up a new girl-friend. It happened in quite a strange way, and I have to laugh now when I think about what I did.

I used to have to go up to the admin office every Friday to pick up my pay and expenses money. There was a very attractive blonde woman called Lisa working there as a finance officer. She was around my age, and I always tried to grab a few flirty words with her.

One day I was standing in the reception of Cyrenians, on the dog-and-bone, when Lisa came down the stairs on her way out of the building. I told the person on the phone, 'Hold on a minute', and beckoned Lisa across to me.

The flirting had all been leading one way, and when she came over, I went for it and kissed her. On the lips. Lisa looked surprised but not displeased – well, she didn't slap my face, anyway! 'To be continued!' I said and carried on my phone call. She and I went for a coffee the next day, had one or two evenings out, and started seeing each other.

Lisa was the first white girl I had ever dated, but that makes it sound like more of a big deal than it was. It just hadn't worked out that way before. Our colours weren't an issue for us or our friends. Why should they be?

Not everyone was so tolerant, though. Lisa and I went out to one or two black clubs and events in Oxford where she wasn't well treated by some people. They were not very welcoming so she didn't want to go to those places any more.

Well, so what? Who cares? We moved in together to a flat on the outskirts of Oxford, near Headington. We both loved music so we spent the evenings playing records. At weekends, we would go to the cinema. Everything was hunky dory.

I was still getting joy and satisfaction from my work at the Cyrenians and I fell a little bit in love with one particular resident. He was an old Scottish guy called Arthur, who was originally from Inverness, and he did not give a flying fuck about *anything*.

Arthur was in a wheelchair and had no family at all but he appeared utterly unconcerned about those facts. He used to point at the carrier bag that was always by his bed. 'All my possessions in the world are in that bag, Jay, lad!' he'd tell me. 'That's all I have, and all I need.'

Arthur and I really bonded, to the extent that he wouldn't do some of the more – shall we say – *personal* tasks we had to do with any of the care staff except for me. And one of those intimate tasks was being there while his catheter was changed.

Arthur used to ladle sugar into his cups of tea like he was using a shovel. He would have four or five heaped spoonfuls in each cup – it was unbelievable! He would get so full of sugar that he couldn't piss and his piss bottle would lie on his bedside table, unused, gathering dust.

The sugar would bloat Arthur's belly out in front of him like a basketball and, every few weeks, a doctor would come around and put a catheter in his dick to let the piss out. It was quite spectacular – as the urine came out, you could watch his stomach deflate like a balloon.

Arthur used to take it all in his stride and never

complain, which was why it was so weird one day that he was wincing in his wheelchair as a young female duty doctor knelt on the floor in front of him to insert the catheter. I even heard him mutter to himself: 'Ow!'

'Are you OK, Arthur?' I asked.

'It's hurting my willy, Jay,' he groaned.

The doctor heard our exchange and started. 'Oh, I'm so sorry!' she said. 'I forgot to put the KY gel on!' She had been trying to push the needle up Arthur's jack's eye without any lubricant! She started fiddling in her bag for the jelly . . . and, without any warning, Arthur started pissing.

He started pissing like a horse. Or maybe an elephant! It was a Niagara Falls of thick, lurid orange treacle. It was totally out of Arthur's control, and it drenched the helpless doctor like some kind of mad, perverted golden shower. The poor woman was too shocked to move.

'Sorry, hen!' said Arthur. He looked at me, I looked at him . . . and we both cracked up. It was impossible not to. The doc looked traumatized, but even she had to laugh later, once she had washed and got cleaned up. It had been pure slapstick.

The hostel used to arrange days out for residents, and I got sent to a little town in mid-Wales with Arthur. The demographic there was even whiter than Oxford, and I had hardly got Arthur out of the minibus and started wheeling him around the streets when the racial abuse started.

'Oi, you black wanker!'

'Piss off! We don't want *your lot* here!'

Passers-by were openly saying the N-word to me! I bridled, but even I knew that abandoning Arthur in his wheelchair and running around thumping the locals would not be a good look. Then Arthur summarized events with a little old-school, unreconstructed racism of his own.

'Ah, ignore them, Jay!' he advised. 'You're a good man, you are. What the hell do they know, anyway? They're just a bunch of stupid Welsh gits!'

The cool thing was, despite all that racist shit, we had a really nice day.

Really, everything was rosy in my garden. My only minor gripe with my life was that I was too far from my family. I was spending a lot of my weekends driving to Luton to see Levi. Justin had also just had a son, Aaron, and I wanted to help my family keep an eye on him.

Luton is just about within commuting distance for Oxford so I suggested to Lisa that we move more that way and drive in to Cyrenians together each morning. She agreed, so I scouted around and found us a nice little flat in a suburb of Luton called Stopsley.

We moved out of Oxford, I returned to Luton . . . and my life once again began hitting the skids.

6

Going forth and multiplying

GETTING BACK TO LUTON INITIALLY FELT GOOD ON A few levels. It was nice to be near Mum and Justin, and great to be close to Levi again. Maria would often bring him and Justin's lad, Aaron, to stay with me and Lisa at the weekends.

On the weekdays, Lisa and I had to be up super-early because it took us more than an hour to drive over to Oxford for work. I didn't mind: I've always been a morning person so I took it in my stride. However, things at Cyrenians were taking a distinct turn for the worse.

I had been working at the home for more than four years by now and they had beyond question been the best times of my adult life. But all of a sudden there were big changes at the hostel that I didn't like. It was getting a lot less caring and a lot more corporate.

The management had a major shake-up and started

cutting corners everywhere. It grew more bureaucratic and suddenly us care workers were being hassled to spend a lot less time each day talking to people like Roy and Arthur and looking after them. It was bollocks, and I wasn't afraid to tell the bosses so.

I'd go up to the office and give them a mouthful on behalf of the staff and residents, and I started having a lot of, shall we say, *heated discussions* with the managers. They really didn't like that. Our relationship got well toxic and it was only going to end one way.

In truth, I can't even remember if I resigned from the home or they fired me. I think it was probably a mix of the two. When I left, in 1994, I knew I wouldn't be missing the management there but it was a wrench to say goodbye to a lot of the residents. They had become friends.

Even after I left, I still had a connection to Oxford because I had started doing some community work in my spare time. I got involved in an organization called the Oxford Education Development Centre (OEDC) that put on various community projects around the city.

I'd been inspired to do this by Sandra, my politically aware Rasta friend from Cyrenians. Her kids, Malachy and Ayesha, and two of their friends helped me to organize an uplifting event on one of the roughest council estates in the city.

The Blackbird Leys was notorious. It had recently seen rioting and anti-police violence that had hit the national headlines. To counter this negativity, I had the idea of organizing a Family Day on the estate. The OEDC gave us some funding and we talked to local elders about it.

On a sunny day, in the middle of the estate, we gave out

prizes for best grandmother, best father, best toddler, what have you. My old mate DJ Spoony was by now a star on Radio 1 and he came down to spin a few tunes. It was almost like a mini-festival and it went really well.

So that was cool, but mostly I was now at a loose end in Luton while Lisa was still commuting to Cyrenians. The dealer guys that I used to know were still around, and while I worked out my next move, I picked up doing a few local weed deliveries for them again.

Why not? It was easy money, all very casual and low level, and I was always far too careful to get caught. However, that didn't stop me falling foul of the law.

Justin wasn't nearly as discreet as me going about his business and he had a few run-ins with the police. He didn't want them going to Mum's house and so, unknown to me, he developed a bad habit of giving the cops my address rather than his when they nicked him.

The first I knew of this came very early one morning, when I was in bed with Lisa and the police signalled the start of a raid on our place by booting our front door off its hinges. It was a total shock but the cops weren't interested in my pissed-off protests.

They found a little cannabis I was supposed to be dropping off to some geezer that day. It was such a tiny amount that they only charged me with possession for personal use, but I had to go to court. I got a £50 fine and a conviction that, I'm happy to say, remains the sole item on my criminal record.

Then Lisa and I finished. We had been drifting apart for a while, and the fact we were no longer at Cyrenians together exacerbated it. There was no one incident that caused the split, and we didn't have a big bust-up. I guess we had just run our course.

It wasn't a clean break. Lisa was proper tight with my family by now. She often socialized with Maria, and when we split up, she moved into the spare room in my mum's place! Talk about complicated – it was like an episode of *EastEnders*!

It meant we were still seeing each other around – and *old habits die hard*. I might bump into Lisa at Mum's, or she might come over to see me of an evening. We weren't *a couple* now, sure, but one thing would lead to another, and we'd end up spending the night together.

Sex with the ex. Well, we weren't the first people ever to do that!

I was twenty-four years old, single, out of a job and in need of earning some money. So, for want of anything better to do, I signed up with the biggest employer in Luton. I went to work at the Vauxhall car plant.

At the time, this enormous factory dominated the town. It produced thousands of cars per week so there was always work going for manual labourers. They took me on to work on the production line.

Shit. I had gone full circle back to the frozen-sausage factory!

I knew it was a backward step from Cyrenians. There, I'd been helping people, getting involved in their lives and hearing about the rich fabrics of their personal histories. By comparison, Vauxhall's was like watching paint dry. It was *so* tedious.

I knuckled down, like I always had at jobs, but the car plant was a weird place. For one thing, it seemed to be unofficially segregated. I couldn't help but notice that all the white workers stuck together, as did the blacks and the Asians. The canteen looked like apartheid South Africa!

An example: I worked alongside a middle-aged white geezer, fixing the linings inside the car roofs as they came down the production line. I have no idea if this guy was racist or not. He never said anything to me to indicate that he *was*: he never said anything to me at all! We could go all day without exchanging a single word.

And now I was back in Luton, another unfortunate element from my past made a very unwanted comeback. *The fighting*.

Newly single, I reconnected with my cousins and my old mates from my previous spell there and started going out partying and clubbing again. And I realized that, during my absence in Oxford, Luton had got no less racist.

There was still this hardcore of white, working-class blokes who didn't like blacks, and I was still just not going to put up with them. If I was out with my crew and the racist name-calling started, I would be in their faces just like I was at Highbury Grove: *BANG!*

I still had the same technique I had had there: *Why didn't you hit him first?* Maximum violence with minimum notice. I went out to have a good time, not to be aggressive or to start trouble – but if trouble *did* start, I made sure that I finished it.

One night, we all went to a pub disco in Dunstable. I met a girl and we had a bit of a chat and a dance. I got separated from my crew, and I was just leaning against a wall talking to the girl when I heard a voice behind me.

'Shut up, you black cunt!'

Excuse me? I turned around to see that, yes, the big white geezer *was* talking to me. He had a couple of friends with him and they didn't look happy that a black guy was in their local and chatting to a white girl.

'What do you want?' I asked him.

'I want you to fuck off, you black cunt! What you going to do about it?'

The guy had clearly assumed that I was on my own. He couldn't see my gang of mates gathering behind him. One of them smacked him – *THUMP!* – on the back of the head, and as he turned around, someone else mullered him. He went down like a sack of potatoes.

It turned out the white blokes had a few mates with them as well and it all kicked off. It was like a Wild West saloon in that pub in Dunstable for a minute or two, but a lot of the racists were all mouth – *they normally are* – and we saw them off.

I remember, as we were leaving the pub, a white guy that I didn't know approached me. 'You know, mate, you should be fighting professionally,' he said, approvingly. 'Not in a ring: backstreet fighting or cage fighting. You're bloody good, and I can see you love it!'

It was hardly a compliment – but the sad thing was that he was right. I wanted a quiet life, but if it was in a good cause, whether it was Iqbal's glasses or sorting out racist thugs, I *did* enjoy wreaking retribution. I *did* still love fighting.

And I was still bloody good at it.

I had called a temporary halt in Luton to tracking down any more of my unknown half-brothers and -sisters, but I was still talking to Sandra and the ones who she had already introduced me to. So, I was pleased when my brother Michael, from Harlesden, called me up with an invitation.

Michael had just had his first kid, Dwayne, and he wanted me to come to the christening. 'I'd love it if you could, Jay!' he said. 'It would be great to see you!'

'Of course, bruv!' I replied. 'I'm there!'

'Our dad is coming as well!' Michael added.

'Cool!' I told him. 'I don't get on with him, but I'm fine with him being there. If *you* want him there, I'm happy for you.'

Two weeks later, the day came around and I got suited and booted and headed down to northwest London. The christening was all good except for one notable absence – there was no sign of The Man Who Contributed Towards My Birth.

Michael and his girlfriend asked us guests back to their house afterwards and Michael went to phone his dad to see what had happened. I'm not sure exactly why, but I followed him into the next room. I found Michael on the blower, looking well disappointed.

'OK, Dad, I understand!' he was saying. 'Yeah, I know you're busy, don't worry about it! I don't mind!' But his face told a different story.

A red mist descended on me. I grabbed the phone off Michael.

'You know what?' I asked TMWCTMB. 'You are a wasteman!'

The voice on the other end of the phone suddenly got very angry.

'Who this talking?' he demanded.

'It's Jay!' I said.

'Jay? Who you think you talking to, boy?'

Boy! He should not have said that!

'You shut your mouth!' he continued. 'I am your father!'

'You should be here, man!' I said. 'Michael's waiting for you. We're all waiting for you!'

'You don't tell me what to do! Show respect for your father!'

I didn't even think through what I said next. The words just poured out of me, with a crystal clarity fuelled by years of resentment and anger.

'I can tell you whatever I want because you ain't nothing to me,' I said. 'I don't even know you. You've never been a father to me. You've never been responsible as a father and now you're not even responsible as a grandfather. *You ain't nothing!*'

The voice on the other of the phone had suddenly gone quiet.

'Why do you have all these kids and not function for them, man?' I demanded. 'Who do you think you are? Why have all of these kids and not take care of them?'

Until my dying day, I will never forget what The Man Who Contributed Towards My Birth growled back at me down that phone line.

'Man must go forth and multiply!' he said.

Man must go forth and multiply! I had nothing to say back. No words. I just shook my head. 'I ain't got time for you no more,' I told him. 'We're done.' And I handed the phone back to Michael.

I was not to talk to TMWCTMB again for a very, very long time.

And it made what happened next all the more ironic.

By now, Lisa had moved out of Mum's spare room and got herself a flat on the Marsh Farm Estate, but she was still tight with all my family. One Saturday, I said I'd babysit Levi and Aaron at Maria's place, while Maria and Lisa went out shopping.

I was playing with the boys when they walked back in later. I could tell that something was up. Maria came in first, and gave me a look I hadn't seen since she and I were together in the eighties and she had caught me cheating on her. It was a look that said: *You've fucked up, mate!*

Eh? What had I done? But Maria didn't say anything.

Lisa was all smiles behind her, and looked happy enough. We all had a cup of tea and I offered to give Lisa a lift back to Marsh Farm. We had no sooner fastened our seatbelts and pulled away when she dropped the bomb.

'I'm pregnant.'

What . . .? I nearly swerved off the road. I was totally dumbfounded. *How . . .?* Well, I kind of knew *how*. Lisa and I had still had our sex-with-the-ex thing going on, and I'd made a few visits to Marsh Farm since she had moved there.

Yet when we were together as a couple, Lisa had always handled the birth-control side of things, and I'd assumed she was still doing that. She'd certainly never said anything to me to indicate that she wasn't – although obviously I should have checked. Man! I was certainly wishing now that I had done!

'But I don't want to have another kid!' I said. 'You know I've got Levi and I'm not with his mum. Now you're telling me this, and you and me ain't together no more either! It makes no sense!'

'I want this baby,' said Lisa.

My next words came from my heart. 'Lisa, I don't want to be like my dad, scattering kids all over the place!' I said. *'I'm keeping it.'*

And that was it. There was no more conversation to be had. It seemed that I had gone forth and multiplied again, even though it was the last thing in the world that I wanted to do. I could have kicked myself for being so stupid and not checking that we were being safe and careful.

Well, it was what it was. And we were where we were.

I wanted to do the right thing so I decided that with a baby on the way, Lisa and I should try and make a go of things again. I moved in with her on Marsh Farm and, as the pregnancy developed, tried to earn some extra cash at Vauxhall's.

The car plant had big orders coming in so there was a lot of night-shift work going. I started taking some on. It was better money and I was just doing the same repetitive tasks on the production line anyway. It made no difference to me whether it was daytime or night-time outside.

It freed up some time in the day to help get ready for the baby, and on 29 June 1995 I was back at Luton and Dunstable Hospital for the birth. It was the same routine as Maria and Levi – the midwives, the gas, the epidurals, the agony – and I was still quietly relieved that blokes don't have to go through it!

But the end result was the same. The midwife handed over a bawling but lovely little mixed-race boy. Lisa and I took him home and we called him Dior. Again, that was mostly Lisa's doing – I was just pleased that it was another short, snappy four-letter name!

I got well into the routine of nappies, burping and Calpol again. It was easier second time around. I knew my way around those jobs by now, plus Dior didn't get the chronic colic that Levi had, so he wasn't as hard to look after.

Maria would bring Levi round to see his new brother, and I've still got photos of them and Aaron sitting in a row together. You would think we were all one big, happy family – but the reality was a different story.

I'd got back with Lisa to try to do the decent thing by her and Dior but it just wasn't happening. We had had problems in our relationship before we split – that was why we had split! – and they hadn't just vanished. In fact, they'd got worse.

I didn't wish Dior away. Nobody with a heart and soul wishes their kid away, and he and I had the same bonding moment as me and Levi had, early doors, when he squeezed my finger in his tiny hand. I loved the little guy – but I also felt trapped, and resentful.

I resented the fact that Lisa had got pregnant when I had had no idea it might happen. It takes two to tango, and I had tangoed with her – but I hadn't known the stakes. Now, I was trying to make a go of us, as was Lisa, but it was doomed.

We had weeks of brooding silences and tensions. Lisa's mum, who had hated me from day one, didn't like her daughter being so far away, and kept on at her to move back to Oxford. She wanted her daughter and grandson nearby and was happy for me not to be part of the equation!

After six difficult months, Lisa and I threw in the towel. She moved back to Oxford, taking Dior with her. And I was once again alone in Luton, feeling lost and wondering what I was to do next.

Around the same time, my mum moved back to Barbados. It was what she had always intended to do after she had made a decent life in England for her and her kids, and I wished her well. I knew she would be happy there. But it just made me feel even lonelier.

Just after Mum moved back to Barbados, I made a music mixtape and sent it to her. It was my usual stuff – reggae, lover's rock, a bit of soul – but when Mum got it, she called me and said she could tell from listening to it that I was sad. My song choices had betrayed me.

It was a proper bleak time for me. Just two years earlier, I had been happy in my personal life and my career had been going great guns at Cyrenians. Now they had both turned to shit – and, worst of all, was I repeating the sins of my father?

Please, no! Anything but that!

Whatever I did next, I decided it wouldn't be Vauxhall's. I'd been at the plant for a year by now and it was doing my head in. I didn't mind the physical labour – it was the sheer, mind-numbing repetition of every shift being exactly the same.

I thought I'd rather take my chances on the building sites again. I left the factory and picked up some more casual labouring work. I had felt like I was getting some direction in life, but now I was back to ducking and diving like an East End wide boy.

This was how I had used to live, but now it felt wrong.

I was older – but was I really any wiser? I stewed, dissatisfied and frustrated. *How the hell had I got here again?*

I had so much self-doubt about who I was, and what I was about, that I even went to see a therapist. My head was in such a fug in those days that I can't even remember who recommended her, but I began seeing a counsellor in Dunstable.

She was a middle-aged lady who lived with her husband but told me that she was a lesbian – which threw me! – and she said she specialized in anger issues. *Sounds perfect for me!* I went to see her once a week in her little home office, sat on a nice sofa and told her about my childhood, my non-dad and my failed relationships.

The therapist murmured sympathetic but quite vague replies and, on my third or fourth visit, we got on to the topic of violence. This was very timely, because my life had recently been getting decidedly violent again.

One night, I had been talking to a white friend in Luton who had passed a disparaging comment about one of my previous partners (I'm not going to dignify the remark by saying what it was, or who it was about.) I was offended by what he said, so I thumped him, which was the only way I knew to settle an argument.

My mate (well, now an ex-mate) went off and told his crew that I had clocked him one, and suddenly there was a whole new gang of white blokes in Luton determined to give me a kicking if they saw me. *Just what I needed!* I had recently had a couple of nasty run-ins with them.

I told my counsellor about these confrontations. 'I think I might have anger issues,' I said. 'Because I have a lot of fights and I get very violent.' She listened carefully then, when my hour was up and I was paying her, she said, 'I'm afraid this was our last session.'

Huh? Why?

'Because of the violence you engage in,' she said. 'I'm won't be able to see you again.'

What? I thought she was supposed to help me solve problems like that!

'Is that how it works in counselling, then?' I asked.

'No,' she said. 'It's my personal decision. I just don't want to work with you any more.'

Blimey, that's a bit much! I went away feeling like a failure, a pariah, thinking that even a therapist wouldn't touch me. I thought there must be something seriously wrong with me.

The building sites were earning me money but I knew I needed to do something more satisfying. Oxford Cyrenians had opened my eyes to doing a job that I loved and that helped people. My initial route into that had been through volunteering.

So maybe I could try that again?

I knew the *Guardian* newspaper had adverts for community work and volunteers in their midweek paper. I could just about read some of them, with help, and I saw an ad for a care home in Luton.

Well, it wasn't really a care home. It was part of the care in the community scheme, and was a house for people with mental-health issues who were being discharged from what were then still called asylums. The idea was to help them reintegrate into society.

I went to see the people who ran the house and told them about my time at Cyrenians. They said they'd love me to help them out and told me a bit about the place. It was, to say the least, an interesting institution.

The managers explained that there were normally six or so residents in the house, who mostly got sent to them from a hospital in Bedford for mentally disturbed people. As a mini-induction, they arranged for me to go on a visit to the hospital.

Wow! If Cyrenians had been an eye-opener, *this* was something else again!

Some patients in Bedford had been in there since they were children. Or they had been sectioned in their teens and never left. I'm not being over-dramatic when I say that being taken around the place put me in mind of Jack Nicholson and *One Flew Over the Cuckoo's Nest*.

One or two patients wore crash helmets because they kept banging their heads against the walls. Others were restrained by being actually shackled to their beds. It looked really disturbing, and I asked the nurse showing me around why they were tied down like that.

'Because they bite people,' she explained, matter of-factly. 'You see that nurse over there?'

She nodded towards one of her female colleagues across the room, who appeared to have a large scar on her cheek.

'She's got a piece of cheek missing because a patient bit it off,' she said. 'And that guy over there has got chunks of hair missing because one of them pulled it out.'

She further explained that other male patients were restrained because they had damaged themselves in a sexual way and couldn't be trusted not to do it again. *Whew! This was going to be quite a challenge!*

Those most extreme patients weren't released to our

halfway house in Luton, but the ones who were had enough of their own issues to be getting on with. It wasn't those poor guys' fault, but it was clear that most of them should not be let anywhere *near* the community. They were chronically institutionalized.

These geezers were in their forties or fifties and had been in mental-health care for decades. They had been bathed, dressed, fed and given their medication for thirty years. Now, suddenly, they were supposed to be able to do it all themselves? *Really?*

I began volunteering in the house in the evenings and at weekends. It was a tough gig. Proper intense. One of the hardest things was trying to stop the men from eating and eating until they made themselves sick.

These guys had spent years being given their meals at certain times, in a very structured way, and now they were in a house where they could wander into the kitchen and take food any time that they felt like it. Given the chance, they'd carry on until the cupboard was bare.

I did a few night shifts there, and I had to keep a real close eye on a guy in his sixties called Michael. If ever he woke up in the night – which he usually did – he would just jump out of bed and make a beeline for the kitchen.

Michael would eat anything and everything. I'll give him this: he was inventive with his cuisine. I'd walk in the kitchen at three in the morning to find him chowing down on dry Weetabix and other cereal, mixed with the contents of a teabag that he had ripped open and scattered on top.

'*Michael!*' I'd say. 'What are you *eating*, man?' But he seemed to enjoy it.

Because we were supposed to be helping these guys to reintegrate into society (or, in a lot of the cases, integrate for the first time), we would take them out into the community for a few hours. It was challenging because they didn't have a clue how to behave.

We would take them to an open-air market and they wouldn't know how to act or to talk to people. They'd walk up to someone, stand right by them and stare at them. If the person got freaked out and moved away, they'd follow and stand even closer.

And these geezers were *strong*! They didn't look physically tough but they knew no fear and, if they wanted to get away from you, they could. I had to be fast while I was out with them, and keep my wits about me.

I got trained in what was called a swan hold: an effective way of restraining the patients. If they kicked off and you started manhandling them, or got them in a headlock, it might panic the public. The swan hold was a little more discreet.

We'd take the blokes to the market and they'd hear noises they hadn't heard in years: police sirens, or the stall-holders shouting. It would set them off. Suddenly, they'd be running around, lashing out, screaming, spitting. *All that good stuff*. That swan hold came in very handy!

Thinking back, I think the care in the community scheme was probably well-intentioned but it was crucial that they picked the right people to try to put back into society. And a lot of the time, as far as I could see, they really, really didn't.

What with the building sites during the day, and the volunteering in the evenings and at weekends, my life was fast turning into an unusual – for me – grind of all work and no play. So, I thought it was fantastic when I got myself a new girlfriend.

I had gone over to Oxford to see Dior and hooked up with some old mates for a night's clubbing. For some reason, I still vividly remember that I was wearing a really nice Ralph Lauren jumper that said 'USA' on the front.

I spotted a girl on the dance floor. She was a really beautiful mixed-race woman with a banging body and wow, could she dance! Her hair and clothes looked immaculate and the second that I saw her, I could not take my eyes off her.

I have to confess, in the days that I was always out and trying to pick up girls, I was prone to the odd corny line. When she came off the dance floor, I strolled over and introduced myself to her by announcing, 'You will be mine!'

I cringe to think about it now, and I certainly wouldn't say anything like that nowadays but, well, *that was just how I was back then*! The woman looked me up and down with an expression that said, 'What a dickhead!' and burst out laughing at my audacious claim, but we began chatting. The more we talked the more I liked her, although I could tell that she certainly wouldn't take any shit.

Her name was Tracey and she was in Oxford visiting friends. She lived in High Wycombe. We had a dance and a good old chinwag, and she was fun and proper feisty. I didn't make her mine that night – *who'd have thought it?* – but we swapped numbers and agreed to meet up again.

Tracey and I had a real spark going from the start. She was still sort of seeing somebody at the time but the relationship was fizzling out and she made a few weekend trips to Luton to visit me. It was a bit of a slow burner of a relationship but after a few weeks, we were a couple.

We got on great and it was very relaxed and cool. Tracey already had a kid, a two-year-old daughter called Leisha. I met her and loved the kid from the start – even though she had a rather unfortunate habit.

Leisha was a lovely toddler who looked as if butter wouldn't melt in her mouth, yet nearly every time I picked her up to give her a cuddle, she would fart. She did it so much that I nicknamed her 'Windy'! I felt so protective of her – as if she were my own daughter.

It was great that Tracey had Windy, both because she was a gorgeous kid and because it meant that her mum didn't want any more children at that point, so I knew she wouldn't be dropping any surprises on me. She and I had been going out for about a year when she made an intriguing suggestion.

Did I fancy moving to High Wycombe to live with her?

I mulled it over. Instinctively, I did. Tracey, Leisha and I were getting on super-well. High Wycombe was equidistant from Luton and Oxford, meaning it would be easy to see both of my boys. And, when I thought about it, there wasn't much to keep me in Luton any more.

The care in the community volunteering had been interesting but it was also draining, and most of the patients were so troubled and far gone that I hadn't formed the kind of friendships that I had with Arthur and Roy at Cyrenians. As for the building-site work . . . well, I could pick that up anywhere.

Inevitably, my natural optimism took over. *Who knows?*

It might even be my next fresh start! I could certainly do with one!

'Yeah, OK!' I told Tracey.

So, there was my immediate plan. My ongoing grand tour of the Home Counties was continuing. I was moving to High Wycombe.

7

Come hell or High Wycombe

I HAD MOVED TO LUTON AND OXFORD COMPLETELY cold. The first day I had set eyes on either place was the day that I turned up to live there. With High Wycombe, I had already spent a few weekends there with Tracey, so I had more idea what to expect.

It was very like Oxford: a well-off area but with pockets of poverty and deprivation. Where Oxford had Blackbird Leys, High Wycombe had an area called Lance Way that was pretty rough and rundown. And that was where Tracey was living.

I moved into her house and we immediately felt like a family. Tracey and I were still rubbing along great and I loved becoming a step-dad to Leisha. She was a lovely kid and accepted me straight away. We all fell into a harmonious life that made me feel good about the move.

The first thing that I did as I found my feet in a new

town was to pick up more building-site work. And it brought me into contact with a level of wealth that I had simply never seen before.

Most of the casual construction work going was in very well-heeled nearby towns such as Gerrards Cross and Beaconsfield. And I quickly found that we weren't going there just to build houses. We were building *mansions*.

Each morning, us navvies would swing through a pair of iron gates and up a long gravel path to our latest assignment. We would get out in front of an enormous country pile, and set about building yet another extension to their existing extensions.

My eyes would be on stalks at the opulence and luxury on display. It was insane. These were some of the wealthiest people in the country and the Georgian facades and Ionic pillars in front of us reflected that wealth. These people weren't messing about!

A lot of showbusiness people lived there because it was convenient for both London and Pinewood Studios. Cilla Black had a place there, as did Bruce Forsyth and Terry Wogan. But I never met any of the residents, because they were never there.

Their estate manager would direct us – 'Please build the cinema room *here*! And the sauna *here*!' – and we'd do the job knowing the owners only lived there for a few months each year. They would spend the rest of the time in their mews houses in central London, or their places in New York or Los Angeles.

I would gawp at the wealth in front of me, and yet I was never actually jealous of it. I would just think to myself: *Fucking hell, these people have really made it!* It was another world completely, and one that had nothing to do with me.

Plus, of course, it was an exclusively *white* world. Over two or three years, I must have worked on fifty houses in that area, and every single owner was white. So were their next-door neighbours. I had never seen a black person be successful in that way.

Well, you can't miss what you've never had – or what you're never going to have.

If my work routine was unexciting, at least my home life was good. Tracey and I had a super-cool holiday when we took Windy – sorry, I mean Leisha! – Levi and Dior to Center Parcs. We felt like a real family. It was a feeling that I wished I'd had a lot more in my life.

I had realized by now that I needed to be doing something rewarding alongside my menial labour. One evening, after work, Tracey flicked through the local paper for me, looking for something that might be appropriate. She came to a small ad and stopped dead.

'Oh, this sounds perfect for you, Jay!' she said.

It was an advert for volunteers for a charity called Youth at Risk that worked with young people who were going off the rails. It turned out the local organizer lived around the corner in Lance Way, so I went off to meet her.

She filled me in. Youth at Risk was a team of mentors who worked with very troubled and delinquent young people. The kids would be referred to them by social services, schools or the police, and they'd work with the kids to try to turn their lives around.

They'd start with local outreach: going to meet youths who had been expelled from school, or were committing crime, to try to persuade them to attend a group meeting. Then they would take the kids to the Youth at Risk residential centre to work intensively with them.

The Youth at Risk residential centre was outside Kidderminster, in Worcestershire. I was keen to volunteer for weekend courses there, partly because it was fascinating, and partly because, at home, Tracey and I had recently started doing a bit of bickering about this, that and, mostly, nothing.

The centre was set in rolling fields, with climbing ropes and adventure play equipment scattered around the grounds. It looked like some kind of scout camp. As I learned on my first weekend there, this was *not* an accurate visual representation of what went on there.

The young people would leap from wooden pole to pole to conquer their fears, and sleep in little chalet-like huts at night. But the primary activity was group meetings in the big main hall – and these meetings could be *brutal*.

They were very intense. Youth at Risk had an American, aggressive, tough-love sort of ethos. The mentors were told to get in the kids' faces and be direct to get a reaction out of them. It was quite confrontational – they were trying to break them down then build them up again.

I wasn't sure about this approach when they explained it to me, but I tried to adopt it. Yet the meetings affected me in a weird way. They were confusing. I kept finding myself challenging the other mentors as if I was one of the troubled young people.

I'd hear the stories these kids were telling about their lives, and they sounded like *my* life. It made me reflect on my own naughty behaviour, and my difficult relationships,

and having had two children so young. It made me realize
– *I did all those things! And nobody tried to help me like this!*

Understanding these kids were on the verge of making
all the same mistakes that I had made me emotional. It
brought a lot of things back to me. There were plenty of
tears shed in those meetings – most of them by the young
people, but quite a few by me.

After my first meeting, the other mentors took me to one
side. They said the reason I had found it so difficult, and
had challenged them so much, was that I had never been
through that level of intense counselling myself. I was
more like one of the young people than I was like them.

They said I was *mirroring*, because I was hearing the
kids' stories about their lives and they were reflecting my
own life right back at me. It was like I was looking in a
mirror.

I could understand what the leaders were telling me,
and I thought they had a point – but there was a welcome
sting in the tail to me being so raw, and having so much in
common with the delinquent youths. It made me really,
really good at mentoring.

It was Cyrenians all over again. Most of the other Youth
at Risk mentors were white, middle class and from privileged backgrounds. Fair play to them, they wanted to help
these troubled young people to improve their lives – but
the kids couldn't relate to them.

The leaders' experience of these kids' world was all
learned, not lived. *They had never been there*. Some were
American, which put another cultural barrier in the way.
One was English but had been trained up by the Ameri-
cans, and had somehow developed an American accent!

It was proper funny. I could see the kids' thoughts on their faces as they listened to him: *You're from England, bruv! Why you talking like that?*

I was different. I knew the hard life they were talking about because I had lived it. *Shit, I was still living it!* When I spoke, I could see the flicker of recognition in their eyes: *This geezer is for real! He knows what we are talking about!* It meant I connected with them very naturally.

And it was just as well that I did – because they were in serious need of some help.

Lee and Kyle were both only fourteen. Lee was distinctive because he was a black lad with piercing green eyes. Kyle had got going on his criminal career early and had already had a couple of spells in youth offender centres, AKA trainee prison.

Those boys were horribly messed up. They both came from broken homes, as did nearly all the kids we dealt with, but that wasn't the half of it. Nobody could get through to Lee and Kyle. They behaved like a right little pair of shits!

Their rap sheets to date included drug offences, robbing people and intimidation. Kyle's bonus speciality was domestic abuse. He would talk quite freely in the group sessions, and one-to-one with me, about slapping his girlfriend around, as if it were totally normal.

After the residential process, the kids got given Youth at Risk mentors to work closely with them back at home. I had a lot of meetings with Kyle and his partner in High Wycombe. We talked about his violence, and I saw the penny drop and him start to get less aggressive.

But it was slow progress, and I perceived a flaw in the Youth at Work ethos. I told the bosses that I thought there was a danger we were breaking the kids at the centre, but not healing them afterwards. We were sending them back to the community broken.

They might open up at the residential weekend but when they got back to the streets, they would revert to their old behaviour of acting tough. It was the same problem: they didn't find the mentors relatable. It was a hard nut to crack.

But Youth at Risk was a good organization and volunteering with them in the evenings and at weekends helped to alleviate the boredom of the daily building sites. Soon, the charity started to notice that I was getting quite decent outcomes with a lot of the young people.

Around the millennium, some of the bosses formed a new offshoot organization called the Kaizen Partnership. They asked me to work with them on various projects, including in a lot of children's homes. I would take a week or two off the building sites and go on location.

I did a couple of mini-stints at children's homes in London. There were some really troubled kids there, but I found it rewarding to hang out with them, listen to their stories and try to connect with them. But I didn't find all the Kaizen jobs so interesting.

They asked me to go and talk to young people working at Nando's. *What the hell for?* Nando's trainees had a job, security and a roof over their heads. I was more driven to help the real underdogs – the kids who had nothing.

Another time, Kaizen sent me to Southampton Football Club to talk to some of the young players in their academy. These were child prodigies who might become future football superstars and they were already on serious wedge.

I had to talk to a group of them, advising them to be careful with their money and think of the future because they might get badly injured, or be released by the club. And I could see in their faces that they had not the *slightest* interest in what I was saying.

I was advising these young guys to keep their feet on the floor but they already thought they were the bee's knees. They were all playing with their phones, yawning and thinking *who is this dickhead?!* They couldn't wait to jump into their Mercedes and go home to play Xbox.

A far more serious – and, in my opinion, more worthwhile – project came when Kaizen asked me to go down to a children's home in Devon.

They had some major problems down there. There had been serious malpractice, with care staff abusing the children, and the management wanted to get professionals and counsellors in to work with the kids and help them to recover from their ordeals.

The strange thing about it all was that I had had hardly any professional training myself. The only thing I really had going for me was my ability to talk and relate to underprivileged kids. And I was certainly going to need it down in the West Country.

They wanted me to work with one particular out-of-control kid. He was only about twelve, but his extreme behaviour had already led to him being thrown out of three or four different children's homes. This place was pretty much his last resort.

Before I left, social services gave me a report on him. I didn't read it. The main reason was obvious – I *couldn't*! If I opened it, the letters still danced in front of my eyes just like they had at Jubilee Primary and Highbury Grove. I had no hope of making sense of it.

However, on another level, I *liked* not reading the report. It meant that I arrived to meet the boy with an open mind. I knew nothing about him, so I couldn't have any prejudices or preconceptions. I thought that was healthy.

When I arrived in Devon, a care worker at the home warned me that the lad was a real handful and said that they had been having chronic problems with him. He showed me to the kitchen and I started making myself a cup of tea as I waited for the kid to arrive.

When he did, he was only a pint-sized nipper but he didn't bother with any preamble or small talk. He ran across the floor, jumped up on the work surface next to where I was standing, and spat in my face.

Well, hello, mate!

I didn't react at first. I didn't even wipe the spit off my face. I let the kettle boil and poured the water into a mug. Then I turned around and grabbed the boy, who was still standing on the counter.

'You should never do unto others what you wouldn't want done unto yourself,' I said. I hawked up a big greenie from deep in my throat – and gobbed it all over his face.

To say the least, he looked a bit shocked. Well, as far as I could see, through the enormous greenie hanging off his forehead.

'Here's how it works,' I said to him. 'You have to learn respect, and you are going to find that I am not like any other care worker that you have ever had. I will do to you what you do to me – so be *very* careful what you do to me.'

The kid nodded.

'I'm going to respect you in the same way you respect me,' I continued. 'So, we can either carry on spitting on each other, or we can start to show each other a bit of respect. It's entirely up to you. You've got spit on your face. I've got spit on my face. Let's see where we go from here.'

I'll never forget what happened next. The lad stared wide-eyed at me, and suddenly all the front and bravado seemed to melt away from him. He was just a little boy again.

'What's your name?' he asked me.

'My name's Jay,' I said. 'What's yours?'

He told me.

'Alright, cool!' I said. 'It seems to me that we might just have a good relationship together.'

I have to admit that it was shock tactics . . . and yet it worked. After that, the lad and I got on great and he behaved beautifully around me – although the care workers told me that he was still a bloody nightmare when I wasn't around!

I did one or two week-long stints with him and a few weekend return-visits, between my labouring work, and then I got asked to go down for a serious matter. The lad had a court appearance somewhere up north and he'd said he wouldn't get in the car to go unless I was with him.

I got sent details of his court case before I went . . . but, again, I didn't read them. *I couldn't.* It meant that what I heard when we got into the court in Yorkshire, where he'd been in a care home before, came as a total shock to me.

It turned out the lad had been sexually abused by the home's staff and had been passed around between them. It had led him to believe that that kind of behaviour was acceptable, or normal, and he had been doing the same things that they did to him to very young children.

Very young children – *and babies*. The youngest victim was just three months old.

Oh. My. God. I couldn't believe what I was hearing. It sent me into shock and confusion. Listening to the court details, I could see logically just why this boy had done what he had. I understood intellectually that he was as much a victim as he was a perpetrator.

Yet on an emotional and instinctive level, I also felt that *I really didn't want to work with him any more*. Just like my therapist had with me, I guess. I was too sickened. The decision was taken out of my hands, because Kaizen put me onto a different project.

It was a gruesome experience and it took me a little while to get over it. If I am honest, on a selfish level, I could have done without it, because it brought me lower at a time when I was mentally not in a good place.

The main reason was that Tracey and I finished. Our rows had come to a head. We had been together for nearly three years, and it was mostly good, but our arguments had been turning into real humdingers – not least because she found it hard to trust me.

Tracey always thought I was seeing other women – and the irony was, although I had often done that in previous relationships, I wasn't with her! I had played around a tiny bit at the start, but been faithful after that. But we had one stand-up row too many and suddenly it was over.

I told a fellow mentor at Youth at Risk, a school teacher called Lisa, that I needed somewhere to live. Lisa had a room to let in her house in a cheap and not-too-cheerful part of High Wycombe called Lane End. I moved in . . . and I took stock of my life.

It was spring 2000 and everybody was banging on about the new millennium and the 21st century. It should have been well exciting, but I felt as if my life was just the same-old, same-old. I was a hamster on a wheel: running fast but getting nowhere.

I had just turned thirty, a landmark age for a man. I wasn't a steady-job, nice-house, wife-and-2.5-kids sort of bloke, but I had always assumed I'd have my life roughly sorted out by this age. *No chance.* I felt like I had nothing. I felt like a failure.

I was getting some satisfaction from Youth at Risk and Kaizen, but I was only an unpaid volunteer there. To pay my bills, I still had to slog my guts out building millionaires' mansions in Gerrards Cross. Seeing that luxury every day was a harsh reminder of how little I had in my *own* life.

I lay on my bed, in my latest rented room, and thought about my string of failed relationships, and my two kids who didn't live with me. *What the hell was wrong with me?*

I wasn't TMWCTMB. I provided for my kids, and I was around for them. But even that was getting harder.

I was still in regular touch with Levi, who was by now at primary school and doing well. But Lisa was with a new man, they had bonded into a family unit, and they always seemed to be busy with Dior. I was starting to lose contact with my second son.

My life felt like a mess; a mistake; a dead-end. *This isn't where I want to be. This isn't the person I want to be.*

I was bemoaning my lot to my landlady, Lisa, one night, not long after I had moved into her house. She looked at me, listened to what I was saying – and had a very left-field solution.

'You ought to go to university, Jay.'

What? I can safely say this was one idea that had *never* occurred to me! Yet something about Lisa's suggestion was so outlandish that it piqued my curiosity. I needed a big challenge to try to turn my life around – what could be bigger than that?!

The local university in High Wycombe is Buckinghamshire New University. I called their switchboard one Monday morning in the late spring of 2000. I could not have been more clueless, or more direct.

'Hello! I want to go to university!' I told the receptionist.

'R-i-g-h-t,' she said. 'I'll put you through to our admissions department.'

A friendly-sounding woman picked up the phone. 'Hello?'

'I'd like to be a student,' I said.

'I see,' she laughed. 'And what would you like to study?'

Oh, bollocks! I hadn't even got as far as thinking about that! What a dickhead!

'Er, what have you got?' I asked her.

'We have hundreds of courses. What are your interests?'

I thought hard. 'I like fashion, and I know a bit about crime,' I said.

'Well, you have two options, then,' the helpful lady said. 'You can study fashion and textiles, or you can study criminology.'

I'd never heard the word before. 'Criminology? What's that?'

'It's the study of crime, and understanding why a lot of

people from poorer areas commit crime,' she explained. Her answer intrigued me. 'Poorer areas?' I asked. 'Like where?'

'Like the East End of London.'

'That's where I'm from!' I exclaimed. 'Yeah, OK, I'll do that!'

The entrance procedure was surprisingly easy. I had a short telephone conversation with a guy from the criminology department. He seemed interested in what I had to say, and said they could offer me a place to start in September. *Wow!*

Then he said something else. He said that he would send me a formal letter confirming my unconditional offer and I would have to send him a reply to accept it. He made it sound very straightforward – which, of course, for 99 per cent of people, it would be. But not for me.

How could I write back to him? I couldn't write – or read! What was I thinking of, trying to go to university when I was illiterate! What the bloody hell was I playing at?

The offer letter came two days later. My landlady, Lisa, who knew that I couldn't read, read it to me. She helped me to fill in the form they had enclosed – but they also wanted an acceptance letter.

'How can I do that?' I asked her.

'Go to the library, Jay!' she said. 'Go on the internet and look up college acceptance letters. See how other people have done it.'

Gulp! But I did. A lady in the library got me on a computer screen and showed me the worldwide web. She found me a letter by some girl in America accepting a place at university and made it so that I could edit it.

OK! Let's do this!

I went through the letter making the most sense of it I could. *Which was not a lot.* It was only a few lines long but it took me an hour to crib from it. The American girl was from Baltimore. I crossed that out and wrote 'Stoke Newington', praying I'd spelt it right.

I printed the letter out, took it home and showed it to Lisa. She said it was OK, and I posted it. A week letter, she read me another letter from Buckinghamshire New University – with my starting date.

Wow! This was really going to happen! I had had a few bizarre twists in my life up until now, but this was beyond a doubt the weirdest of them all.

I was going to university.

8

The teaching ability of a peanut

I'VE ALWAYS BEEN A CONFIDENT BLOKE. SOME MIGHT even say cocky. I feel able to survive, or even prosper, in a new social situation. A mate in Hackney once called me the United Colors of Benetton, because he said I am a social chameleon who can get on with anyone, whatever their colour or background. I like that, and I think, in a way, I am.

But I have to admit it – I was absolutely bricking it before my first day at Buckinghamshire New University.

I knew I was going back to the one thing I bloody hated: *school*. Me and education just hadn't got on. I had loathed the experience of secondary school. And now here I was, going back into a classroom. *Why?*

Well, I was doing it because I knew I needed to make a change in my life. I knew by now I had enough wits and intelligence to get by, but I didn't have any qualifications to prove it. *I was still unclassified.* And it was time to try to rectify that.

I didn't show how nervous I was about the prospect. I put on a front. *I even put on a front to myself.* But, inside, I was shitting myself.

I didn't have a clue what to expect on the first day, but what I *didn't* expect was something called Freshers' Week. I followed some signs into a big hall where lots of perky, cheerful new students were walking around deciding which extra-curricular clubs and societies to join.

They all looked young – *very* young! They were fresh-out-of-school teenagers, virtually all white, very polite, and extremely well-spoken and enthusiastic. They looked like children to me. I walked, bamboozled, around the room with them, and people sitting behind desks waved at me and asked me questions:

'Hello! Would you like to play lacrosse on Wednesdays?'

'Hi! Would you like to go parachute jumping?'

Umm . . . do what? I didn't want to say no to absolutely everything, so I signed up to play basketball one evening a week. I had been OK at that at Highbury Grove. It might even be fun to pick it up again.

I got given a reading list of books for my course. I found the university bookshop and bought a few of them. When I got home and opened them up, my very worst fears were realized.

Shit, these books were intense! They were thick, heavy textbooks with hundreds of words crammed on each page in small print. Just looking at them made my head hurt. There was no way that I could bluff my way through these. I couldn't make head nor tail of them.

Jesus, Jay! What the hell have you done?

My university life proper kicked off the following week. I had a lecture on the Monday morning, so I found my way to the lecture hall and sat myself at the back among all of the eager, bright young things. *OK, so what happens now?*

A middle-aged professor walked into the hall with a pile of notes, put them on a lectern and started reading them out to us in a monotone. His voice was a dull drone – and I didn't have a Scooby what the geezer was talking about.

'The psychology of cross-generational criminality . . . the complex interdependence of causation factors . . . a forensic re-examination of motivation . . .'

Huh?! The guy might as well have been talking a foreign language. In effect, he *was*. Every word he said went a million miles over my head. It was ridiculously highbrow, and I was floundering. *Badly.*

I stared around the lecture hall at my fellow students. Every single one of them had their head down and was writing furiously as the professor spoke. Their pens were scorching over the paper. What were they hearing that I was missing?

'Do you understand what this geezer is on about?' I asked the guy next to me.

'No,' he whispered. 'But I'm just writing down what he is saying and hoping I can make sense of it later.'

'Do *you* get what he is saying?' I asked the girl on the other side of me. She shook her head, and continued scribbling manically.

I must have looked like a meerkat, with my head up and swivelling from side to side in curiosity as everybody else was taking notes, because the lecturer looked up and noticed me. He broke off his talk.

'Are you OK?' he asked me.

'No, not really,' I said.

'And what seems to be the issue?'

'The issue is that I don't have a clue what you are talking about!' I said. The awkward silence in the lecture hall was broken by a few titters.

I must admit that the next thing I said could probably have been a lot more diplomatically expressed, but this was just how it came out.

'Look, mate, you have the teaching ability of a peanut!' I told him. 'You are supposed to take us on a journey. You're a professor, right, and we are all just . . . freshers!'

There were a few laughs in the hall, and I realized that I had probably used the wrong word. But I pressed on.

'You're an expert, right?' I said. 'You've been studying this stuff for years. I'm just an entry-level criminologist and I don't understand what you're saying. I don't think anybody does, but everybody else is too ashamed to say so. You've got to break it down! Put it on our level!'

The lecturer looked astonished, said something I didn't catch, put his head down and resumed droning away. He and I did *not* get on from that day forth. My card was well and truly marked with him.

After the lecture, I milled around and spoke to a few of my super-young fellow students. They were friendly, but they were all full of the course and the textbooks we had to read. One or two of them said they had read half of them already.

Bloody hell! I couldn't even read half a page!

It was the most inadequate and lonely I'd ever felt. I simply thought: *I don't belong here*. Surrounded by these chattering teenagers, I knew I had made a huge mistake. I had taken on way too much. But, well, *here I was*. I had made my bed and I had to lie in it.

The actual course I was taking was Criminology and Philosophy, and the weeks settled into a routine of lectures and seminars. For the first few weeks, I was winging it. Unable to read the books, I'd turn up with no idea what the lesson or tutorial would be about. And yet, despite this, I somehow managed to get something out of them.

The other lecturers were better than the first guy, and if I had got the hang of a topic, I wasn't scared of speaking up in a seminar. I would just listen to what the other students said, the ones who *could* read the books, then chip in and give my opinion. My natural confidence resurfaced.

Some of the criminology course did my head in, though. They told us about Victorian days, and how the police used to think that criminals had certain phrenological character-istics. Basically, if you had bumps on your head, or a broad nose, you were more likely to be a villain.

Huh? How did that work, then?

Initially, it was the philosophy side of the course that blew me away – and that was largely down to one of the lecturers. He was a professor called Trevor Hussey, and he became a bit of a god to me.

Trevor was an unbelievable teacher with an unbelieva-ble brain and he opened up doors for me. *He opened up doors in my own brain*. Trevor would say things in our seminars that had my mind boggling. He got me thinking about life in different ways.

He started off teaching us about the great Greek philosophers such as Plato and Aristotle and the way he talked about them was beautiful. He might say, 'There is no such thing as a true statement.'

Eh? I would interrupt, 'Excuse me, but what do you mean?'

'Everything is always changing,' Trevor would explain. 'If a man says, "There are a hundred white swans in Britain", how does he know he is correct? A swan might have died at the very second that he made that statement. His statement may be false. The person who knows most is the person who knows that he knows nothing.'

Or Trevor might point at a chair and ask, '*Is* that a chair? We assume that it is, because it has the form of a chair – but some chairs are not that shape or design. What if it is not a chair at all, but merely a representation of a chair?'

Woah! This stuff frazzled my brain, but it was exciting, and I longed to learn more. He taught us about Bertrand Russell, and Jeremy Bentham, who said that intelligent people had always manipulated poor people to do their will, from slavery right through to workhouses and prisons.

Yet, more than those specifics, Trevor Hussey taught me the power of argument and discussion. He was the first lecturer at Buckinghamshire New University who got me interested in the course and in learning.

He was the first one who made me think that maybe, just maybe, I might belong there after all.

For a bit of relaxation, I started going to the basketball club I signed up for in Freshers' Week. At least I could shine there! I still remembered my old ball tricks from

Highbury Grove, and the building sites had kept me fit enough to compete with the kids – and to outdo them.

One week we were having a practice session and a woman came and joined in. If I had any doubts if she could keep up with us, they were soon dispelled, because she was running rings around most of the boys! I couldn't take my eyes off her.

Three things hit me in rapid succession:

1) *Wow, she is shit-hot at basketball!*
2) *She's not a teenager – she's about the same age as me!*
3) *Woah, she is incredibly attractive!*

In fact, if I am honest, that is not the order in which those thoughts occurred to me!

She must also have noticed that I was the only other non-teenager on the court, because after the session she came over and spoke to me. We headed off for a coffee in the student bar, and she told me a bit about herself.

Her name was Jade Erguvanli, and she was from the Turkish capital of Istanbul. The reason that she was so good at basketball was that she'd played the sport professionally in Turkey! She had come to England, lived in Brighton and done a fashion course in London before moving to High Wycombe. Now, she was studying textiles.

Jade was two years younger than me, had been married twice, and had a life behind her and a few stories to tell, unlike the wide-eyed kids we were mixing with. She was cool, and exotic, and I knew I wanted to see more of her from the second we met.

In fact, I fell in love with her. I think it was also from the second we met.

Jade had the same bizarre living arrangement at Bucks that I did. I had by now moved out of Lisa the teacher's spare room and onto campus, where I joined an accommodation scheme that the university ran.

The uni liked mature students such as Jade and me to help look after the wet-behind-the-ears kids who had just left home for the first time. They called us senior residents and gave us rooms to live in rent-free – but these perks came with responsibilities.

I had a room in an old pub that had been converted into student accommodation and now housed fifteen students. Another conversion across the road held the same number, and I was responsible for the inhabitants of both of them.

Basically, I was halfway between a part-time warden and a surrogate dad to these kids. If one of the lads rolled home drunk and started kicking up a fuss late at night, it was my job to sort it out. If a window got broken, I had to notify the university. Fascinating stuff like that!

I probably wouldn't have chosen that role voluntarily, but the rent-free room was a major attraction. As I was now living on a student grant and not building-site money, that shit mattered.

Jade had a similar role in a house elsewhere on campus and we'd meet up for a drink and compare the problems we had to deal with as senior residents. If you could call them problems. They certainly weren't mountains. They were hardly even bloody molehills!

A typical vignette would see a polite, posh young lady, on the verge of tears, knock on my room door after breakfast.

'Mark took my cornflakes!' she would sniff, as if it were the end of the world.

The students all either had their own room or were two to a room, but the kitchen areas were shared. There were no locks on the cupboards or fridges so they all wrote their names on their items of food. Which frequently went missing.

'How do you know Mark has taken them?' I'd ask her.

'Because I saw the empty box outside his room.'

'That doesn't mean he took it – anybody could have left it there!'

'No, it was him! I put my ear to his door and I heard crunching!'

Honestly! I used to think, *if you think of this as a crisis, my girl, you have led a very sheltered life!* It was proper comical. I often had to struggle to keep a straight face as I listened to the distraught, cereal-less students.

I felt like saying to them: 'Look, here's £2 – go and buy another box of bloody cornflakes and keep them in your room! Emergency solved!' Instead, I'd go and have a quiet word with Mark, who'd naturally deny all knowledge of the Kellogg's heist. *Ho hum.*

After a few weeks, Jade and I went from being basket-ball-club pals and dinner buddies to becoming a couple. I was delighted. We shared a lot of personality traits – we were both very driven, hyper and motivated. We were like two jigsaw pieces that fitted together.

Jade also started helping me out with my course work, and it was just as well that she did. Because I was strug-gling badly.

I liked the seminars and I could follow most of the

lectures even though I couldn't read the textbooks before-hand. I could grasp the arguments and theories, but everything fell to bits as soon as I had to get it down on paper.

My courses weren't big on written work in the first year, but every time I had to write an essay, it was embarrassing. I could talk fluently to Trevor Hussey about Jean-Paul Sartre, but when I had to write about him, it looked like a child's doodles. My marks were proper shit.

Jade was baffled. She would read me something from a textbook that she found interesting and I'd develop the idea in exactly the same way as the author – and add a wicked twist. She could see I was up to the task intellec-tually – so why was I faring so badly?

Then, one day, she walked in on me hunched over a criminology book, squinting, pointing at the words with my index finger and moving my lips. And the penny dropped.

'Jay!' she said. 'You can't read, can you?'

'No,' I confessed, quietly.

'Right!' she said. 'We need to get you tested for dyslexia.'

I was up for that. I was up for *anything* that would end the mortifying hell of being unable to read. The university had a scheme going aimed at recognizing disabilities and helping students to overcome them. I had a word with them and they fixed me up with an appointment.

I went down to London to see dyslexia specialists. It was like going to an optician. A smart and efficient lady put a book in front of me and asked me to read aloud. She covered one of my eyes, then the other. Then she asked me to read the words through a coloured filter.

I struggled, naturally. It was all quite intense, and shortly after I had finished, she called me into her room to get the results.

'When you attempt to read, we can see from the movements of your eyes that you can't process the words,' she said. 'They dart around as if the letters are moving and your eyes are trying to control them. The colour filters help a little, but not enough.'

'What does it mean?' I asked her, simply.

'It means that you are certainly dyslexic. You have a reading age of approximately eleven. That is the age that you stopped learning.'

As soon as she said the words, they made utter sense to me. *Of course!* Eleven was the age that I had gone to Highbury Grove School! The age when everything had started going wrong for me!

The age when I had stopped learning and started fighting.

It was a relief finally to understand why I had never been able to read. A relief to realize that it wasn't just that I was stupid. And now I'd been diagnosed, the lady briskly explained that there were many things they could do to assist me.

They gave me coloured filters, which helped a bit, but my reading still wasn't great and using them alongside a computer was quite a palaver. What worked far better for me was a life-saving computer programme.

Back at Bucks, my course tutors gave me a piece of computer software called Dragon. It would read me an assignment and I could just talk my answer into the computer. I could then print it out and hand it in as my essay.

Wow! Where had this been all of my life?!

Once I had Dragon, my issues melted away. It read my textbooks to me, I dictated my course work into it, and suddenly I was on a par with the other students. I was no longer unfairly handicapped or held back by the invisible ball-and-chain of my illiteracy. It was a revelation.

Suddenly, university and everything about it made sense to me – and that included the marking system at the end of my degree course, which I had until then been in blissful ignorance about.

A guy on one of my criminology modules was talking to me one day about grades, and mentioned that he wanted to avoid getting a 2:2. I was totally flummoxed.

'What do you mean, you don't want a tutu?' I asked him. 'You wouldn't look good in it!'

The lad fell about, then explained what he meant. He said that most students who put the work in got a second-class degree. The target was a 2:1, whereas a 2:2 was not so good. Only a handful of very elite students managed to get a first.

I instinctively didn't like the sound of a second-class degree (*or, in fact, a second-class anything!*) and I told the geezer I wouldn't be bothering with that. 'I'm getting a first, mate!' I proclaimed. 'It's in the bag!' I was laughing when I said it. But I still meant it.

I threw myself into my studies with a passion. Now, I absolutely *loved* my course. I loved how the philosophy seminars had taught me to how to structure an argument and engage in a debate, and I loved applying that new intellectual rigour to my criminology lessons.

It didn't mean that I liked everything about the course. As I grew in confidence and awareness, I realized that I really didn't appreciate the perspectives that a lot of criminologists brought to their research. To me, they seemed well awry.

It was the nature of the history of study of crime that a lot of it was white, middle-class professors studying poor black people, many of them from council estates. And they talked about these people as if they were subjects, or rather *objects*, and hardly real people at all.

It was incredibly patronizing. The criminologists would discuss the kind of East End council estates I had grown up on as if they were breeding grounds for dysfunction and hotbeds of crime, and nothing more. They talked about them as if they were zoos, and the people living in them were animals. And it made me bristle.

No, bruv, this is all wrong! I would think to myself. *We're not animals on those estates! We love each other and we look after each other. We would die for each other. We might be poor, but we are a community and we have a code. Don't dis us like that!*

Of course, me being me, I generally didn't just think those things: I said them, out loud, in the seminars and tutorials. And now that I had the tools to express myself properly, it made for some really fascinating discussions. I was learning, and I think the tutors were learning from me.

I learned just how long racism had been endemic and systemic in Britain. I'd always vaguely imagined anti-black racism had sprung up in London when I was a kid, but now I realized that it was a structural, historic phenomenon that reached back for decades and more.

Wow! I got a real big awakening. It was enlightening and disheartening to realize just how much injustice had been dished out to black people for so many years. It made me begin to think, *shit, this stuff is still going on today! Why hasn't it got any better?*

I was beginning to fear that the history of criminology was essentially racist – but then the cavalry arrived. We began learning about the work of two major black criminologists who, not surprisingly, delved into the topic with a lot more understanding and empathy.

Professor Ben Bowling talked about the chronically flawed policing of the black community. I could relate to that! And Professor Stuart Hall, a Jamaican academic, coined the phrase 'the moral panic of mugging' to describe the anti-black racism routinely whipped up by the tabloid press.

It was such a fillip to read those guys. They inspired me and liberated me. *Yes!* I thought. *I can definitely connect to this!*

I got inspiration from a black academic closer to home when I took a module in film studies. The professor, Dr Martin Patrick, had a really direct and powerful teaching style that had a massive impact on me. I had a bit of a secret hero-worship thing going on for Dr Patrick!

At the end of my first year at Bucks, Jade gave up her role as senior-resident wet nurse for the young students and moved into a flat near the campus. I held on to the job but was basically living in her place. I got to know my sparky new partner even better.

Jade was from an educated, middle-class Turkish family but she was also a bit of a rebel. She was spirited and independent and, despite her own privileged upbringing, she had a strong feeling for the world's underdogs and a natural sympathy for ethnic minorities.

Jade had turned that sense of injustice into a fervent

desire to *make the world a better place*. I recognized it as the same drive that made me want to do volunteering and community work. Like me, she was always questioning stuff. Always driven.

It was funny – in some ways, especially our backgrounds, we were so far apart that you wouldn't have thought that we belonged together. But in other, more important ways, we were kindred spirits.

Jade and I had earnest, heated discussions deep into the night about unfairness and inequality and racism. They were intense, and passionate, and sometimes they turned into arguments, but they were always exciting and stimulating. We got a lot out of them.

We made a very potent and powerful connection. We realized we both wanted to be a force for good in the world. And then, suddenly, we got the chance to do it – because the police came calling.

In my earlier life, when the police came calling it was not good news. *This was different.* A community worker from the Oxford Education Development Centre, who had helped me to organize the Blackbird Leys family day, got in touch and said that a very senior officer was asking about me.

Chief Superintendent David McWhirter of the Thames Valley Police had heard about the family day and my community and volunteering work. He wanted to talk to me about how his force were policing ethnic minorities, and how they could do it better.

Hmm. My previous interactions with the police had not been great, to say the least. But this seemed like a genuine offer: could it be an opportunity? I talked it over with Jade and decided to hear him out.

I met Chief Superintendent McWhirter in a community hall in Oxford. He seemed a nice guy and told me that he had heard good things about me. Then he asked me the sixty-four-million-dollar question: *how did I think the police could do thing better?*

Ha! I let him have it with both barrels. '*You're doing everything wrong!*' I told him. Tell your officers to treat black people as human beings, not as suspects. Tell them to say 'Hello!' to us when they go past. Tell them not to look at us as if they assume that we're about to commit a crime.

Tell them not to stop and search us for no reason. 'Imagine if every time you went to a shop, the shopkeeper followed you around in case you stole from it,' I said. 'Well, that's how black guys feel, walking down the street every day. And it's you, the police, that make us feel like that.

'You work for the community,' I concluded. 'But the problem is – you're hated by half of the community that you work for.'

I doubt that a black geezer had ever had the chance to speak to David McWhirter like that before. Credit where it is due, he loved it. He said it was just the sort of thing he was trying to correct – and he asked me if I would help him to train his officers.

Do what?! He was asking me to police the police?

He was. Chief Superintendent McWhirter explained that he wanted me to address a meeting of superintendents and sergeants, and repeat to them all the things I had just said to him. Then he wanted me to help them to improve matters. And he would pay me to do it.

'How many police will be in the meeting?' I asked.

'About forty.'

My head was in a whirl. My innate distrust of the police kicked in. *I'm a black geezer from Hackney! OK, I'm in university now, but I haven't got a qualification to my name and, unknown to this guy, I've got a history of violence and low-level drug dealing. Can I really do this?*

At the same time, David McWhirter seemed totally on the level. He was giving me a lot of credit. And this kind of opportunity didn't come along every day. In fact, it didn't come along *ever.*

'OK, I'll do it,' I told him. 'Where will I be talking to them?'

'In the police station.'

Uh-oh! We fixed up for me to do it, but I was still wary. The night before I was due to go in, I was talking to an old mate from Hackney on the blower. He couldn't believe what he was hearing.

'*You?*' he laughed. 'Going into a police station to train the police?'

'I know, I know,' I said. 'Crazy, innit? I don't know if I'll make it out of there again! But I promise I won't be grassing anybody up.'

'Don't worry, Jay,' he said. 'If I don't get a call from you the day after, I'll know that they've banged you up!'

It was a jokey conversation but, well, like they say, *many a true word spoken in jest . . .*

The police station meeting went well. I told the officers about my bad experiences with the police and what I thought needed to change. They had a lot of questions, took notes and seemed to be listening. They even let me out of the station again at the end!

Chief Superintendent McWhirter was at the meeting

and he said that he thought it was brilliant. And he had another, even more daunting yet exciting proposal for me.

The Chief Super asked me to join his force's independent race relations advisory panel – and he wanted to commission me to oversee a major project. He wanted to try to improve race relations in four of the most deprived areas of Oxford. And he asked me how he should do it.

Wow! That was one big question right there! I went away and talked to Jade about it. We did some research, talked to a load of kids on the streets and then presented David McWhirter with an ambitious plan.

We suggested that we would organize workshops for young people in Blackbird Leys, Barton, east Oxford and Rosehill. We would talk to them about their grievances with the police, give them questionnaires to fill in and feed the info back to the police to act on.

David McWhirter instinctively liked the idea and said he'd commission us to do it. He agreed to pay us for our work. But I still had another demand.

'OK, we'll do it,' I told him. 'But we'll be using these young people as consultants, so we need to pay them, as well. I want to give them £5 each for taking part.'

'I'll see you get the money,' Chief Superintendent McWhirter said.

Blimey! Jade and I went away with a task, a budget and a million thoughts in our heads. It was thrilling but also vastly intimidating: *How are we going to do this?* I had just learned that I had a reading age of eleven: how the hell could I compile a complex questionnaire asking disaffected youths to critique the police?

This was where Jade came in. I told her the questions

that I thought we needed to ask the young people and she translated them into a great questionnaire to prompt them to share their experiences, and tell us the areas they thought the police could improve in.

Ha! How about every single one? I thought.

Jade also had major input on the questionnaire's appearance. We both knew a list of questions on a clipboard would look boring to the youths and put them off. It would look like schoolwork. It had to be visually engaging to grab their attention. She had a great idea.

We met a pair of graphic designers and explained her concept – that the questionnaire should stimulate the kids' imaginations and have a load of folds that they had to open up to find the questions. Every time they lifted up a corner of paper, there was another question.

The two designers did a great job and the questionnaire was a work of art. It looked like a beautiful piece of origami. Not that Jade and I thought it was so beautiful when we had to sit up for hours late at night folding hundreds of the things!

It was all getting very time-consuming and I realized the project was so big that there was no way I could do it alongside my existing university studies. I spoke to the criminology and philosophy department heads, who both agreed to let me take a year's break from my degree course.

We put the word out, the police publicized the scheme and Jade and I began setting up the workshops. We advertised four of them in each of the project's four areas and a lot of kids told us they were going to come. The fact they were getting a fiver for turning up definitely helped!

The workshops were fascinating. The racial mix that

turned up differed in each area. Blackbird Leys was mainly black, Barton and east Oxford mostly white, and Rosehill a real mix, including Asians. But the story coming back loud and clear about the police was the same everywhere.

I would always open the meetings by asking how the youths felt about the local police. The answer never varied.

'*Fuck the police, man!*' they'd tell me. 'Fuck 'em off! We don't need them! Get them out of here!'

'Well, OK,' I'd say. 'I agree there are some wrong 'uns in the police. But what if your granny got kicked in the head and robbed for her pension? What would you do then?'

'I'd sort it out myself!'

'But if you do that, you might get messed up and get in serious trouble. Wouldn't it be better to have the police to sort them out?'

'I suppose so . . .' they would concede, thoughtfully.

I'd probe deeper to find their root grievances against the police, and the answer was always that they didn't trust them. All the black and Asian kids had been harassed by them, and a lot of the white ones too. There were kids there as young as twelve who had horror stories.

We would talk for an hour and then some police officers would come in for the last hour of the session. I told the young people they could ask the cops anything they wanted to – and they certainly took me at my word. There were scores to settle.

'*Why did you stop me on the way home from school last week?*'

'*Why did you arrest me for loitering when I was doing nothing?*'

'*Why did you nick my weed, man? I don't know what*

happened to it – did you smoke it in the police station?' (I had to laugh at that one!)

'Why didn't you give me a Dipsi form when you searched me?'

This was a regular complaint. The police were supposed to give every kid they stopped and searched a form called a 'Dipsi' which was an official record of the search. Oxford police had not been bothering. When the youths challenged them at one of the workshops, the cop just said: 'I dunno why. I think our stationery supply ran out.'

This went beyond mere paperwork. If the Dipsi system was working, it would show the vast over-representation of black youths being stopped by the police compared with white ones. Not filling in the forms meant the info was lost. Which was rather handy for the coppers!

Some of the officers bridled at the questioning. I could see they didn't like the kids challenging them. But the beauty was they knew we had the authority of their chief superintendent behind us. They had to just swallow it.

We got amazing feedback. As well as more than a hundred kids coming to our workshops, eight hundred filled in the questionnaire! We took their feedback and answers and Jade compiled them into a report to Chief Superintendent McWhirter, making a list of recommendations.

We said that local schools should hold similar workshops, aimed at under-sixteens, and police officers should attend. We suggested that young people who had come to our meetings could help to arrange them. McWhirter agreed to these ideas – and he went a step further.

In our workshops, the names of a handful of police who were abusing, harassing or even beating up kids had come up repeatedly. We gave them to the Chief Super – and he called those officers in, reprimanded them and moved them away from those beats.

Wow! Not only was I helping to train the police – I was even getting the rotten apples disciplined and kicked off their patch! I could hardly take it in. I would never have believed it was possible that something like this could happen. It felt ground-breaking: incredible.

It might sound funny, but Chief Superintendent McWhirter was a fairy godmother in my life. He took a big chance on me when I was a nobody with no credentials, no credibility, and nothing going for me except a voice and a sense of injustice. And he helped to turn my life around.

David McWhirter was delighted with our report and said he wanted Jade and me to do a lot more work for him. And we wanted to do it. In fact, we were *gagging* to do it.

This was what Jade and I had dreamed of in our fervent, passionate discussions deep into the night. The chance to do some good in society. The chance to make a difference in people's lives. We had got lucky. It had fallen into our laps, and we were going to grasp it with both hands.

We wanted to formalize the work we were going to do and make it into an entity: a brand. We wanted to give it an identity. We needed a name, and one day we were discussing this with my friend Sandra's kids, Malachy and Ayesha, when Malachy came up with a corker.

'Why don't you call it Street Dreams?' he asked.

Street Dreams! We loved it the second we heard it. Because that was what we wanted to do – to take people from the streets and help them to realize their dreams.

Help to make them a reality. We wanted to find underprivileged, down-beaten kids and give them a leg up.

We called ourselves Street Dreams and we gave the name a strapline: *A fresh approach to stale problems*. Because there were so many stale old problems around: racism, police brutality, inequality, you name it. And we were going to look for brand-new solutions to them.

It was exhilarating and I couldn't wait for me and Jade to get our teeth into the next big project. But in the meantime, I had the little matter of a university course to finish.

Jade had already graduated because I had taken a year off to work on the police project, so she shouldered a lot of the Street Dreams weight as I threw myself into the final year of my degree. If anything, the time off had helped my learning. I didn't feel like an entry-level criminologist any more!

I wrote a dissertation that I called *Manufacturing a Black Criminal*. It argued that society conspires to feed young black men into the criminal justice system, to which they are just so much product. I argued that it was similar to the slave trade – incendiary stuff!

When it came to my final exams, my trusty Dragon software came to my aid as usual and let me express my knowledge and ideas without having to write them down. I must have made a half-decent job of it because I graduated with a 2:1.

I must admit that I felt a little disappointed that I didn't get the first I had been banging on about . . . *but only a little*. Shit, the last time I had picked up exam results, I had been staring at a single letter repeated over and over on the wall at Highbury Grove: U U U U U U U.

I had gone into the world unclassified. Now I had a B.A. (Hons). How could I not be chuffed? And at least I didn't have to wear a tutu!

My mum flew back to England and came to my graduation ceremony with Jade, and told me she was proud of me. I was quietly proud of myself, too, but I wasn't about to wallow or rest on my laurels. I was way too impatient to get on to the next thing.

Because Jade and I were ready to take on the world with Street Dreams.

9

Lions and Mongolian prisoners

I HAD GONE INTO BUCKINGHAMSHIRE NEW UNIVERSITY clueless, floundering and not knowing what I wanted to do with my life or even which course I wanted to study. I left with a sense of purpose and on a mission.

I felt like a more serious, *bigger* person. Now I had a goal and I could envisage a proper place for me in society. For years, I had been like a Scalextric car with no track, revving my engine with nowhere to go. Now, I suddenly had a course to drive down. I had a purpose, and a direction.

All of my experiences, from Youth at Risk through my degree and the police project, made me realize: *Wow! I can talk to people! I can make a change in their lives, for the better!* For the first time, I felt respected for something other than how handy I was with my fists.

It was a new feeling, and I liked it very, very much.

After Street Dreams' success in Oxford, Chief Super

McWhirter passed our details on to a police chief in Banbury. This guy asked us to improve some troubled race relations in the town, where there had recently been bad disturbances between white and Asian youths.

Jade and I visited the town and began to formulate a plan to tackle its issues. And I began to realize just what a shit-hot partnership we could become in Street Dreams. Right from the start, she and I were a dream team.

We came at problems with the same passionate desire to solve them – but from totally different directions. Our skill sets were a million miles apart and yet utterly complementary. There is no other way to put it: we were yin and yang.

I approached things on a totally street, gut level. I knew what I wanted to achieve but I wouldn't necessarily know how to organize stuff to make it happen. I could talk to angry young people, on their level, and I could get through to them, but authority figures were difficult for me.

Jade was the exact opposite. She was sophisticated and charming and professional and she saw the big picture. She could communicate with the officials and local authorities and get them on board. She could draw up our bids, write the reports and quantify what we were doing.

We came from different worlds but when it came to community work, we quickly became a power couple – a match made in heaven. *Jay and Jade: even our names seemed to fit together*. And this unlikely pairing began achieving some pretty amazing results.

In Banbury, I started talking to the young people on the streets but Jade and I knew it was also important to get the elders on board, particularly in the Asian community. So, I went to the mosques to pay respect to the elders there and establish a dialogue with them.

Some of the older imams didn't want to know and denied that there was any problem with their young people. They laid the blame for the racial tension firmly at the door of the white kids: *No, no, our Muslim youths are not troublemakers!* It was hard to make any progress there.

The younger mosque leaders were different. They were more realistic, and pointed us towards the ringleaders of the aggro on the Asian side. And I managed to get a conversation going both with them and with the biggest troublemakers among the white kids.

I was basically saying the same things to both sides. I told them that a lot of the violence was because they were bored and frustrated and had no facilities. They were blaming each other – but the real problem was the authorities were giving them nothing to do.

I explained to them that the local council hated the fighting and rioting because it was putting Banbury in a bad light. If they came together and spoke to the authority with one voice, they would be in a really strong position and the chances are that they would get what they wanted.

And I asked them the all-important question, the one that nobody had taken them seriously enough to ask them before: *What is it that you want?*

It varied. The Asian kids were keen on being allowed more access to the local sports and football facilities. A lot of the white youths wanted the skateboard parks to be better maintained. The concrete was cracked, and they were falling over and cutting themselves on broken glass.

Jade and I organized workshops in Banbury, as we had in Oxford, where the kids came together and itemized their grievances. It showed the white youths and Asian boys that they had a lot more in common than they'd thought.

These meetings were a great forum. They increased the mutual understanding between the two ethnic communities a hundredfold and they realized they had no need to be at each other's throats. The trouble on the streets soon fell away.

Of course, it wasn't all plain sailing. *It never is.* Our meetings got pretty high powered, and at one we had the head of Banbury Police, the chief executive of Oxfordshire County Council and the leader of Banbury Council. The kids elected a couple of spokesmen to talk to them.

One of the white lads was a grungy-looking skateboarder who looked like he was off one of the council estates but was actually from quite a well-to-do family. He made a plea for one particularly neglected local skate park to be fixed and given some tender, loving care.

He didn't get much of a hearing. The head of Banbury Council brusquely interrupted him and told him that the council didn't have the funds to renovate that skate park. And the grungy kid came straight back at him.

'That can't be true!' he told him. 'Your council has just spent £150,000 planting flowers on every traffic roundabout in Banbury. Are you telling us that our lives are worth less than flowers?'

The leader of the council went red in the face. 'How do you know that?' he spluttered. 'Those figures are not public information!'

'I volunteered at the local council office and I read the info there,' the lad said. 'Now, what about our skate park? How about fixing the public property where we are falling over and hurting ourselves?'

The chief councillor was so livid at being challenged that he walked out of the meeting and he wouldn't let Street Dreams do any more work in Banbury. But he couldn't undo the good we had already done. It was another triumph for Jade and me. And more kids' problems solved.

I was totally focused on Street Dreams. It fixated and consumed me. It meant that I was completely interlocked with Jade both professionally and personally, and it made our relationship absolutely different from any that I had been in before.

Put simply: I had zero interest in other women. It never even occurred to me to try to play around. To explain it in Scalextric terms again: when I was a kid, the track always had stands and crowds on the side: little things that you'd put there to make it all look a bit more realistic.

You never looked at them because you were too busy flying your car around the track, and that was what I was like now. Any other woman, no matter how attractive, was like a Scalextric tree or a pit mechanic: decorative, but destined to be ignored.

Jade and I might have a meeting with a female community worker or volunteer, and afterwards Jade would tell me, 'I don't like that woman.'

'Why?' I'd ask, puzzled. 'What's wrong with her?'

'She was flirting with you!' Jade would say. 'Trying it on!'

'*Was she?*' And I would laugh my bloody head off.

Because I genuinely had not even noticed. I had retired from that game. And I was glad that I had.

Jade and I got bedded in closer and closer. Our long conversations into the night continued and got ever more intense. Jade was always hyper-focused on finding a way forward, past or around any obstacle that might present itself. She was all about *development*.

'*This* idea has worked well,' she would say, as we planned and plotted Street Dreams. 'But how can we take it forward from here? How can we *develop* it?'

Jade applied the same rigorous process to me. She was fascinated by the differences in our upbringings and how they had shaped our contrasting views of the world. She would challenge me on every front, and question my views on life, society, the police, racism . . . everything.

I don't think it's too exaggerated to say that Jade *challenged my whole existence*. She challenged me to step outside of my experiences and see the world in a fresh way, and made me realize how blinkered and narrow-minded I could still be in certain situations.

Occasionally, I might resent her interventions . . . but on the whole it was an exhilarating feeling. Jade, and Street Dreams, were developing me as a person and I could feel myself growing. I loved it. And I loved her.

She took me to Turkey to stay with her parents in Istanbul, and wanted to show me everything about the city in one single visit. It was insane. We were running around that busy, crazy capital non-stop, trying to look at a million things at once. The heat was unreal.

Jade had an interesting relationship with her parents, particularly her dad, Ali. He was Turkish and her mum,

Heather, was English. They had first met at university in London and then her mum had moved to Turkey with him and they had got married.

Ali was a civil engineer and had raised Jade to be independent and a critical thinker. She was, but she had a very different philosophy and attitude to life from him, and the two of them frequently butted heads over their differing outlooks.

I hardly met her dad. We stayed with them but Ali was never around when I was there. I suspected it might be because I wasn't a doctor or a lawyer or an academic, but it wasn't that. It turned out later that her parents were not getting on very well.

Heather was completely different. She was warm and understanding and welcoming, and I liked her a lot. But even in their house, I got insights into Turkish society and how it had turned Jade into the firebrand that she was.

Her parents had a lady who came in to help them run the house three days per week. I would wander into their kitchen to make myself a cup of tea, and Jade's mum would come in and gently scold me.

'No, no, Jay!' Heather would say. 'Zeynep will make your drink!' And she'd summon the home help to do it for me. I always cringed and felt a bit awkward when that happened. I like to make my own cup of tea.

Turkey is full of exotic splendours and Jade wanted to initiate me into the world of reiki. I didn't know a thing about it but one thing about me is that I've always been game to try a new experience, so Jade took me off to meet a female reiki grandmaster.

Reiki is all about energy flow and auras, so this lady was sitting in front of me, moving her hands around me without touching me, freeing up my chakras and my inner energy. She didn't speak a word of English so Jade was acting as our interpreter.

The grandmaster was getting well intense with her movements and talking to Jade in Turkish as she waved her hands. She must have been opening my chakras *right* up, because suddenly I could feel a strange energy flow through the channels inside me – and I could see stuff.

Weird stuff!

'Shit, Jade, I can see really bright colours!' I said. 'And lions! Loads of lions!'

'Yes,' said Jade. 'That's exactly what the healer is telling me that *she* is seeing!'

Woah! It freaked me right out. I wasn't scared, but it was really weird. That lady opened up my chakras too far, because as Jade and I went through the hubbub of Istanbul's streets in a taxi after my session, I was seeing all kinds of crazy shit out of the window.

I could see lions and rainbows, and among the crowds I saw strange, vividly dressed people that I knew weren't really there. It freaked me out and I told Jade about it. 'Take me somewhere calm!' I said. 'I need to be somewhere where I'm not seeing this stuff!'

We went to a Four Seasons hotel, which was nice and chilled, but as we sat drinking tea, I glanced out of the window. *Huh?!* I saw Ottoman Empire soldiers herding Mongolian prisoners. I'd never been to Istanbul before, and suddenly I saw its entire ancient history unfolding before me.

Bloody hell! It was too much! It was fascinating, but also deeply unsettling. I had Jade take me back to the woman to close down some of my chakras again, because it was doing my head in. You know what? Life is complex enough without lions and Mongolian prisoners!

Back in England, a police superintendent who had worked with me and Jade in Banbury had now moved on to Milton Keynes and brought us in to do some work on the Lakes Estate in Bletchley. It was to be one of the most challenging projects Street Dreams ever took on.

The Lakes had been built at the end of the sixties and housed a lot of building workers who were constructing the new town of Milton Keynes down the road. The Greater London Council part-financed the estate so they could use it for London's population overspill.

The GLC told their problem tenants and nuisance neighbours: 'Look – you're being evicted! And the only place we're going to offer you is in Bletchley!' So, a load of working-class white people, a lot of them with nasty, racist attitudes, moved en masse to the town.

It gave the Lakes Estate a serious racism problem. This was next-level stuff. Academics had been studying the estate for thirty years to see why it was so racist and not been able to do anything to fix it. I had never seen anything like it.

Racist people had moved in and raised racist children and now racist grandchildren. Most of the violence was whites beating up Asians. The estate had been almost exclusively white until a few Asian families had moved in, and then all hell broke loose.

Local care workers took Jade and me to a road where a lot of Asians lived. Every window and car down the street had been smashed. Leon Comprehensive School, in the middle of the estate, was a big conflict point. A lot of little Iqbals were getting their glasses broken there.

Whew! We were taking on a major job here! And yet, in a strange way, I felt confident.

Street Dreams got brought in by a multi-agency mix of the police, the local council, the parish council, social services and youth services. The youth services people didn't like us, because we'd basically come in to do their job. We had a lot of red tape to cut through.

At the start of the project, Jade and I gave a presentation to representatives from all of those bodies. There were thirty people sitting around a table: everybody from senior police to nursery nurses. I made an impassioned pitch to them about what we aimed to achieve.

'Look,' I said, 'we are going to be able to change this community in three months. It is going to happen and you need to be ready for it!'

There were a few sniggers. 'Christ, *you're* confident!' someone said. I saw a lot of sceptical smirks exchanged around the table. When I asked for a show of hands at the end, only three of the thirty people in the meeting thought we'd be able to make a difference.

Jade and I did exactly the same things that we had in Banbury. I went out and found the local community leaders and ringleaders, on both the white and the Asian side, and I talked to them.

'The way that you lot are all conducting yourselves – you're setting yourselves up to fail,' I told them. 'You need to tell me what it is that you want and I'll guarantee you that it will happen.'

I don't think they knew what to make of me at first. 'Really?' they asked, suspiciously.

'Yes! The council have brought me in from the outside because they want to make things better here. *You* want the same thing. So, you need to tell me: what do you want to change? What do you want to see in your community?'

And Jade and I listened to them.

At our meetings, we asked the youths what they were interested in. It was the same stuff as all youths: music, football and girls. We started fixing up activities that could bring the two warring tribes together. Because *that* was the main thing that would make their lives better.

We set up a football match on the estate, but we made sure it wasn't Whites vs Asians: it was two mixed teams. We started a boxing club. We set up a radio station for them, and then hired a camera crew and filmed a music video. The council supported us all the way.

I wanted to make the two communities understand each other and emphasize their similarities to dilute the hostility. There were St George flags all over the estate so we talked to the Asian kids about St George's Day, and what it means to white people. We tried to open their minds.

And it worked. As the understanding between the two communities grew, the tensions dissipated and the conflicts fell away. It happened amazingly quickly. I had told the local authorities that Street Dreams would make a difference in three months. It didn't even take that long.

Jade and I had been active in Bletchley for two months when the local police started coming up to us in the street.

'Bloody hell, what are you two doing to our young people?' they asked. 'There's no anti-social behaviour any more. There's no crime. We've got nothing to do!'

It was great to hear because it showed that we were doing things right and getting results – but we hadn't waved a magic wand. We hadn't pulled any slick tricks. We had just gone there and done what nobody had ever done to these poor people before. We'd listened to them.

The Street Dreams work was coming in thick and fast. Jade and I did a project in Jericho in Oxford, where back in the day the local council had actually built a wall around a council estate to segregate it from the wealthy people! We also did some work in Wolverton in Milton Keynes.

While I was driving home from Wolverton one evening, my back went into a full spasm. It turned out I had a ruptured disc and it was agony. It meant that I had to stop driving long distances for projects – so Street Dreams began to look closer to home.

Jade and I were really keen to do projects around our own home area of High Wycombe and Buckinghamshire. There were plenty of young people hanging around High Wycombe with nothing to do, so we got to work there.

We had done one project already. There had been an issue with black youths beating up white BMX bikers and skateboarders and stealing their money. We had got some funding off the council, went to see the young people and asked our usual question: What do you want?

The skateboarders wanted to hold a battle of the bands for rock bands and the black kids wanted a grime contest for MCs. We managed to get them working together and put on a joint event that was a bit of both. It went well, so the council were open to more collaborations.

It was important for me and Jade to try to train up some of the young people to be the next youth leaders. We sent them on courses. It was part of our philosophy: *we wanted to work ourselves out of a job.* Because we knew when she and I were fifty, kids wouldn't relate to us! We wouldn't be cool then!

Street Dreams took on a project in Lane End, the poor part of Wycombe where I had rented the room from Lisa the teacher before I had gone to university. I walked into the first planning meeting . . . and unexpectedly saw a familiar face.

It was my first-ever lecturer from university – the guy that I had told he had the teaching ability of a peanut! He did a right double-take when I walked in the room, and didn't look at all pleased to see me. I could read the thought bubble over his head:

Bloody hell, it's that mouthy student who gave me a hard time and called me a peanut! What the hell is he doing here?

He looked awkward in the meeting because it became clear that he was there to pontificate airily about why kids might turn to crime, whereas *we* were there to try to make a practical difference and improve things right here, right now. Which is what we did.

Everything was bowling along super-nice in my life. Jade and I were still joined at the hip and Street Dreams was going from strength to strength. Back in Luton, Levi was working hard and had just left school and started college to study electrical engineering. I was proud of him.

The one fly in my ointment was that I was losing touch with Dior. He was still in Oxford with his mum, Lisa, and my chances to see him were still few and far between. I heard on the family grapevine that he was causing trouble in his primary school and had been threatened with expulsion, although in the end that didn't happen.

Not seeing Dior was frustrating, but I had so much going on in my life every day that I let it slide. I could have pushed harder for access to him, maybe even gone through the courts, but I didn't. I wish now that I had done.

Jade was still working hard at my personal development. She liked to expose me to different environments that I wasn't used to and see how I coped, and in 2006 she came up with an absolute doozy. She sent me on a training course at Henley Business School.

This was a seriously upmarket institution and, if I am honest, I felt like a fish out of water. I sat around a table with besuited captains of industry and listened to them talk about management techniques and optimization of resources. I felt like it had nothing to do with me.

We were worlds apart. I had a business, sure, but it was a business that was about trying to make communities better, not maximizing revenue and corporate profit! I listened to the executives speak, and I thought their concerns were insignificant in the grand scheme of things.

The one interesting part of the course was that we all took Myers-Briggs tests. These were questionnaires designed to discover what kind of personalities we had and thus what sort of leaders we were. We filled in questions about ourselves and they took them away to mark.

That afternoon, the woman in charge of the session

came back with the results. 'We have a lot of extroverts in this group, which is what usually happens, because that is the nature of the business world,' she said. 'But we also, unusually, have an extreme introvert.'

We were all looking around the table, trying to figure out who it might be. There was one very quiet geezer who had hardly said a word, and I clocked him looking self-conscious. *Yeah, it'll be him!* I thought.

'It's Mr Blades, from Street Dreams!'

What? Really? I was amazed, and I listened as the woman said that I had scored as such a spectacular introvert on the test that she was surprised that I was there at all.

'Whose idea was it for you to come on this course?' she asked me. 'It wasn't yours, was it?'

'No,' I said. 'It was my partner's.'

'I thought so! You don't really want to be here, do you?'

'No!' I confessed, to laughter around the table.

Two of the course leaders thanked me for coming, and congratulated me for joining in with everything even though it couldn't have come naturally to me. 'You do a lot of community work, yes?' one of them said. 'And you influence a lot of people?'

'I suppose so,' I replied.

'It must exhaust you,' he said. 'You're so far out of your comfort zone, because you're an extreme introvert who is behaving like an extrovert. What you are doing in communities is admirable – but you will need to take breaks, or you will do yourself harm and burn yourself out!'

Hmm. I was gobsmacked by all this at first but the more I thought about it, the more it made sense. After a full day of community work, I always had to get home, relax and have some 'me' time. I needed to chill out.

Jade was the total opposite. She was more of an extrovert, and would be firing questions at me as soon as I got in, wanting an inquest straight away: *OK, how did it go? What worked? What didn't? What shall we do next?* Whereas I needed to switch off, put on some John Holt, reflect and recover.

So, yeah. Maybe those geezers Myers and Briggs were on to something, after all!

But Jade and I were still firing on all cylinders and we were about to find ourselves pulled even closer together. Because, all of sudden, we discovered that she was pregnant.

The idea of us having kids had come up before, but we had always quickly dismissed it. We just figured *we don't have the time*. We were married to Street Dreams, 24/7 – how the hell could we take on all of these huge community projects and also juggle childcare?

I wasn't even sure Jade would take to motherhood – she was all about targets and goals and achievements, and had never shown even the slightest hint of feeling broody. Yet when it happened, she and I just looked at each other and smiled.

We both said the same thing: *'Yeah. Let's do it. It's time.'*

On 17 June 2006, we packed Jade's overnight bag for High Wycombe General Hospital and I psyched myself up for a third viewing of my least favourite action scene: childbirth. It was fairly quick, and the familiar sound of baby cries soon filled the air . . . but this time it was different.

It was a girl.

Blimey! In a funny way, having a daughter knocked me sideways. It felt somehow different from when I had Levi and Dior. I had looked after Leisha when I was with Tracey, and loved her, but now this vulnerable, tiny creature was my own flesh and blood. I immediately felt incredibly protective towards her, in a totally new way. I had a thought running through my head from the second I set eyes on her:

A daughter! This is serious shit now!

We called her Zola (yep, another snappy four-letter name!) and I was totally wrong about Jade and motherhood: she was a brilliant, doting mum from day one. And now we had become a three-person unit, I felt another, immediate imperative: she and I should get married.

It's probably a bit old-fashioned, but I had an instinctive feeling that a father should be the sort of man that he'd like his daughter to marry one day. And the first part of that stature was actually being married to her mother. Jade liked the idea, so we fixed a date.

Before that, we took Zola to Istanbul so Jade's parents could see her, and I even got to hang out with Jade's dad as Ali spent a bit of time in the house to meet his grandkid. In Barbados, my mum was delighted about Zola. After Levi, Aaron and Dior, she finally had a granddaughter!

Jade and I married just a few weeks after Zola was born, in a registry office in a local hotel, Danesfield House. It was cheap-and-cheerful because we had no money, and there were only twelve people there, but it was a nice day.

We didn't have a honeymoon. We had a one-day break, then we were straight back to Street Dreams.

We were still focusing on Buckinghamshire and doing a

lot of work in schools. We went into one secondary school in Chesham, where I got talking to a gang of Asian teenage boys who had started not doing their work and being disruptive in lessons.

I gave them a mood board and asked them to draw their futures. Three of them drew big mansions – the kind I used to build in Gerrards Cross – with huge pillars and flash cars outside, and Rottweilers guarding the gaff.

I asked them how they intended to get the money to finance this ultra-bling lifestyle. 'We'll be gangsters!' they told me. 'We'll get bitches and put them on the street! They'll work the street and make money for us.'

These boys had been watching too many rap videos! They were just silly teenagers bragging, and it might even have been funny, like *The Inbetweeners*, but I could see they were in danger of going off the rails and messing up their lives.

'You know if you're going to be a gangster, you'll probably go to prison, right?' I asked.

'Ah, prison's nothing!' they said. 'We know people who've been inside and they say it's pussy stuff! We can handle it!'

'Oh, yeah?' I replied. 'Have any of them ever told you how they got raped in jail by six older men?'

They looked shocked. 'No!'

'Well, they wouldn't *admit* it, would they?' I asked. 'But that stuff happens! Pretty boys like you wouldn't last ten minutes in there!'

They looked a bit unsure but like they still didn't believe me, and their bravado soon returned. So, I decided to teach these wannabe pimps and gangsters a life lesson.

I arranged for them to go on a nice little day trip to

Huntercombe Young Offenders Institution near Henley-on-Thames. I spoke to the jail staff beforehand and asked them to treat the boys exactly as they did the inmates. 'Don't go easy on them!' I urged. 'They need to learn!'

When we got to Huntercombe, the warders made the boys change out of their designer threads into jail uniforms that had been worn by God-knows-how-many lags before them. They took them to the canteen and gave them some of the stale slop that the young offenders were eating.

I could see the boys' eyes growing wider. *Shit, this isn't like it is in the rap videos!*

I introduced the schoolboys to a couple of young but already grizzled-looking inmates spooning down their lunch. 'You're lucky you weren't here yesterday, buddy,' one of them said, not even looking up from his plate. 'A guy got his eye gouged out.'

'*What?*' asked one of my lads, terrified.

'Yeah, man! A gang fight broke out, and we popped his eye out!'

'Didn't you try to stop it?' my boy asked the warder who was showing us around. The guy just laughed.

'Why should we?' he shrugged. 'If these fuckers want to beat the shit out of each other, we let them! We don't give a fuck. We let them hurt each other for a bit, and then we bang them up in their cells for twenty-four hours.'

The Chesham teens fell very, very quiet. They didn't say a dicky bird in the car all the way back to school. They stopped being disruptive in class, and I never heard another word from them about putting bitches on the street to finance their mansions. *Job done.*

Back home, watching Zola grow up was amazing. It was so unlike being a dad to the boys. There was no kicking a ball here: right from her toddler years, she was totally into the little-girl stuff of glitter and frills and princesses. She loved placing golden crowns on my bonce.

Somebody told me a saying: *You're not a dad until you have a daughter.* It's true, because I instinctively became hyper-protective towards Zola – and one reason for that was seeing other young girls getting used and abused as we did our Street Dreams work.

This was the era of the rise of mobile phones, when any kid could get on the internet and see anything – including pornography. Going into schools in Buckinghamshire, Jade and I met too many boys who had been taught by porn that they could do whatever they wanted to girls.

The schools would refer individual naughty kids to us, and one head teacher asked Jade and me to talk to a thirteen-year-old girl. He said she was acting up in class and was often late for her lessons with no excuse.

She seemed a sweet kid when I met her, and I asked her my usual opening gambit: 'You OK? What's going on with you?'

'I'm alright,' she said.

'The school say you're getting to your lessons late?'

'Yeah, I am,' she admitted.

'So, why's that?' I smiled. 'Do you find it hard to get out of bed in the mornings?'

'No, I'm *always* in school on time.'

Huh? I was puzzled. 'So, if you're in school on time, what's the problem with getting to your classes?'

'I have to do sex things,' the girl said. 'I give blow jobs

179

for 20p at break times. There is always a queue of boys I have to get through before I can go back to lessons.'

Whew! Where do you start with something like that? As well as telling the teachers, the main priority for Jade and me was helping that girl to regain some self-respect. 'You don't need to do that,' we told her. 'Take more care of yourself. You're far too good for that.'

We found other horror stories of boys passing girls around, and these terrible attitudes were being inculcated by internet pornography while the lads were still proper young. Now and then, Street Dreams went into primary schools and met with kids whose families were not great influences.

I gave a talk to some primary kids and then took them to McDonalds for a reward. One of the kids had a little doll, and after he'd wolfed down his burger, he put his doll on the table and started flicking ice cream all over her.

FLICK! FLICK!

The lad was aiming at the doll's face but it was going all over her body. Not to put too fine a point on it, it looked like he was trying to spunk on her. *Man, I hoped I was wrong!*

It was important not to just come down on these troubled kids and say, 'Stop doing that!' so I watched him carefully for a few seconds before asking him, as casually as I could: 'What are you doing?'

FLICK! FLICK!

'It's what the men do when they stand around the lady,' he explained. *Bloody hell! I wasn't wrong!*

'Where did you learn that?' I asked him.

'From the videos that my brother watches . . .'

Oh. My. Days.

I was from the streets but, even so, Street Dreams taught me things that I had not even known were going on. When I was a kid, guys like me and Iqbal had to watch out for gangs of white boys going 'Nigger-bashing' or 'Paki-bashing'. It was one of our hazards of growing up.

Now, Jade and I found gangs of Muslim kids, some of them still primary-school age, who had had enough of being beaten up for their parents' faith. They wanted to get some revenge. They were going out *Christian-bashing*.

They'd find some little white lad, playing innocently with a ball in the park, and surround him.

'What's your religion?' they'd ask him.

He'd have no idea what they were on about: 'Eh? What do you mean?'

'What religion are your mum and dad!'

'I don't know! Sorry!'

'Ah, he must be a Christian!' And they'd give him some nasty beats. Jade and I had to do a lot of work trying to turn around attitudes like that.

Street Dreams shoved some of the very worst sides of modern society, some of the most delinquent kids, right in our faces every day – and yet usually, after the initial shock, it didn't get me down. I still felt positive because I knew that Jade and I would be able to turn things around. To make things better.

I knew we would be able to make a difference. Which was all that we had ever wanted. And, nearly every time, we did.

In February 2010, I turned forty. We had a massive house party in High Wycombe with a marquee in the garden, and a lot of my old mates from London, Luton and

Oxford came up. It all got a bit lively, and the police arrived to ask us to keep the noise down, but it was a cracking evening.

Forty is another landmark age for a geezer, but it didn't bother me. I looked at my life and I felt *happy*: far happier than I had at twenty or thirty! I felt as if my life was on the right Scalextric track. I was pleased with where I was going.

It's funny how often that feeling precedes things taking a bit of a downturn.

10

Urban types collecting stuff like Wombles

EVER SINCE CHIEF SUPERINTENDENT DAVID McWHIRTER had asked us to police the police in 2001, Street Dreams had always had a steady flow of work projects. There was no shortage of broken youths and racial tensions out there, and we were constantly being called in to repair them.

We were running a few youth clubs. Parish councils would see bored young people hanging out on street corners or vandalizing stuff and pay us to set up a club for them. After a while, we would depute the kids we had sent on training course to oversee the clubs' day-to-day running.

But then things changed. Work had got a bit scarcer around the global financial crash of 2008 but we had survived that.

Then in 2010 there was a change of government in Britain and overnight our funding began drying up. The new coalition government seemed to have decided that the people who should pay for the crash weren't the financial speculators and the bankers who had caused it, but ordinary people – especially those at the bottom of society. They started pulling the plug big time on council funding.

Suddenly local authorities hardly had the cash to keep the schools going and empty the bins, let alone hire outside specialists and consultants such as us. One by one, Jade and I saw the funding for our projects fall away.

Austerity hit the charity sector hard. The big traditional charities such as Oxfam and Barnado's still got their slice of the pie, but young, upstart organizations like Street Dreams suffered badly. 'I'm sorry, we'd love to hire you, but we just can't afford it any more,' councils were telling us.

The need for Street Dreams was as great as ever but Jade and I began to wonder if it was still financially viable. We knew we wanted to carry on – but we were badly in need of a Plan B.

It was Jade who came up with it. With her background in fashion and textiles, she was also steeped in furniture design. She was a regular visitor to charity shops looking for bargains, and as we cast around for alternative projects, inspiration struck her.

Jade had the idea that we could teach young people to renovate old furniture. We could pick up tattered chairs dirt cheap from second-hand shops, rub them down, give them a lick of paint and put some new fabric on them, and sell them on. *Hey presto! Instant profit!*

I had zero knowledge about, or experience of, furniture restoration in my life up to this point and, if I am honest, my first response was that it simply wouldn't work.

'Nobody is going to want to buy second-hand furniture, Jade!' I said. 'I just don't see it! But you have never been wrong so far, so if you're sure on this one, I'll be guided by you. Let's give it a go.'

Jade came up with the name Out of the Dark. It was partly because we hoped to bringing light into people's lives, but also due to the fact that we would be lugging old furniture out of dark attics, cellars and store rooms. And we rolled up our sleeves and got to work.

Jade and I didn't wind up Street Dreams. It was still going, in a lesser form, but we transferred a lot of our attention to this new project and began touring the charity shops of High Wycombe buying up old chairs and cupboards. They were so cheap that it was a joke.

Our beginnings couldn't have been more rudimentary. Jade and I stuck four tall fence posts in the lawn in our back garden and chucked a tarpaulin over them to make a primitive work space. I took the ancient sofas and chests of drawers in there and began to sand them down.

It wasn't hard to find young people to get involved. Schools were still referring individuals to us, and because Street Dreams was fairly well known in Buckinghamshire by now, quite a few worried parents sent their kids to us direct. It was all via word of mouth.

By now, Jade and I had identified the core principle behind Out of the Dark. It wasn't so much to teach young people to restore old furniture, because that would sound boring to them. It was to teach them how to turn something that looked to be worth nothing into an item of value.

So, when the first few kids came and stood in our tarpaulin workshop, I piqued their interest. I said:

'I'm going to show you how to make money from nothing.'

They looked at me, well sceptical. 'Huh? Nobody can do that!'

I pointed to a knackered-looking old chair, its stuffing hanging out of the sides. It was a pile of junk they would normally have ignored, or smashed up for kicks if they were bored.

'That is £175, sitting right there!' I said.

'What?! For *that* piece of shit?!'

'Well, not like it is now!' I laughed. 'You've got to bring it back to life first!' And I explained how to strip it, rub it down, paint it and put new fabric on it. *£175!* The boys suddenly looked a lot more interested.

I could do the basics but I was no furniture-restoration expert. It was crucial to bring in people who were. We wanted Out of the Dark to be a true community venture, so I went in search of members of the older generation to teach these young people their skills.

We went to the local Women's Institutes and Neighbourhood Watch groups, asking if they knew any restorers . . . and we got super-lucky. I hadn't fully realized this before, but it turned out that, historically, High Wycombe was steeped in furniture. In fact, it was the furniture capital of Britain.

There had been many great manufacturers and companies based in the town over the decades, from Ercol to G Plan and Parker Knoll. It meant that when I went in search of older people who might be willing to share their knowledge, there were a whole load of them.

I heard about a ninety-two-year-old guy named Ken, an ex-policeman who had also worked caning chairs. He was now in a care home in Beaconsfield and said he'd love to help. However, the home wouldn't let him come to our garden workshop because of health and safety.

So, when a kind person donated six broken cane chairs to Out of the Dark, I took the kids to the care home and we sat around Ken in a shed as he showed us how to fix them and told us his old police war stories. The chairs were a hundred years old. Ken made them look beautiful again.

A lady called Rose, who used to work on the Queen's Royal Collection, came to help. She told us how, after World War II, a lot of caning was done by blind people who worked by sense of touch. Good old Rose was such a fast caner! Her hands were a blur.

A company named Green Gate, who had been making furniture in High Wycombe for four generations of the same family, taught us how to do traditional upholstery. They had always made very high-end furniture, including all of Ralph Lauren's stuff in Europe.

While I was up at Green Gate with some youths, the father of the guy who owned the company said, 'Let me give you a little history lesson.' He pulled out a book that was like an encyclopaedia of furniture over the ages. It had pictures of some of the most beautiful chairs and sofas I had ever seen.

That book made a huge impression on me. The guy explained that back in the day, furniture makers dressed incredibly smartly because they took such pride in their work. I took that philosophy into doing my own restoration work. Looking smart helps your frame of mind.

I found I was a quick learner and I picked up the rudiments of furniture restoration quickly, but far more important was how readily most of the young people who got sent to Out of the Dark took to it. Once they got the hang of it, I could see it was giving them a real satisfaction.

These were kids who had been told from an early age – like me – that they were thick and would never amount to anything. Some couldn't read or write, but when they sanded down an old chair properly, and I said, 'Beautiful job, man!', I could see their faces glow with pride.

I realized that furniture restoration was a metaphor for their lives. Even at this young age, they had already been written off and cast aside by their schools, or by society, or even by their own families. Well, with a bit of care and attention, worthless things could become valuable.

Just like them.

They liked learning the skills and I knew it was impor- tant that I didn't just order them around, saying, 'You're doing it wrong – no, do it like *this* instead!' Sometimes I'd play dumb and make a mistake on purpose, so they could put me right. It gave them a sense of empowerment.

Out of the Dark was coming together and I could see that the young people loved being involved. Jade and I divvied up the workload the same as in Street Dreams: I handled the frontline stuff and Jade talked to the authori- ties and sorted out the finances, contracts, PR, etc.

The first clue I got that we might have a viable business model came when Jade managed to get a picture of one of our restored chairs into a major design magazine, *Architec- tural Digest*. An Italian geezer got in touch via the magazine and offered to pay top dollar for it.

Ker-ching! Result! As I sat in our tarpaulin cave wrapping up this chair that had been fit for the tip a few weeks earlier, in order for it to be couriered to Italy, I smiled to myself. *You know what, Jay?* I thought. *Jade might be right! We might just be on to something here . . .*

By now we had too much second-hand and donated furniture stacked up in our garden tent to be able to work in there. Jade and I started casting around and looking for a decent-sized workshop that we could rent in High Wycombe.

We found a semi-derelict old workspace and made a verbal agreement with the owner that we could rent it. Jade and I spent days washing out the place, chucking out crap and scraping off pigeon poo – at which point, the guy reneged on the deal and decided to keep it himself!

We should have charged the scheming git for our cleaning services but we took a deep breath, wrote it off to experience, and found a new, perfect space to rent. And, as we moved in and Out of the Dark picked up steam, I was delighted that an aching gap in my life got filled.

After a year or two of little contact, my ex-partner Lisa in Oxford phoned me up. She was worried about Dior, who she said was still causing grief, and was in the last-chance saloon at his secondary school. Lisa was at her wits' end and asked me if I could get involved.

Dior was a good kid but at this age – in his mid-teens – he was a bit like my brother Justin when he was growing up. He was a thrill-seeker and so he didn't always make the best choices in life. I was relieved to hear from Lisa, and delighted to be asked to help him.

'Of course I will!' I told her. 'That's what I do nowadays – I help kids to turn their lives around. I'm hardly going to say no to my own son!'

After I had talked to Dior, I got an appointment with the headmaster at his school. When I went in for the meeting, I laid my cards on the table.

'This is the situation,' I told the head. 'I haven't been in Dior's life for a while, but I am now. What can we do to make things better?'

The head raised one eyebrow and handed me a folder of Dior's school behaviour notes across the desk. He almost needed two hands to lift it. As I flicked through, he filled me in on my second son's transgressions.

There were a lot. Being rude in class, arguing with teachers, truancy, fighting, smoking in school, not doing his work . . . it did not look good. The headmaster confessed that he was inclined to exclude Dior from the school for good.

'Please don't do that!' I said. 'I'm going to get on top of things with him and I will communicate with you every week – every day, if you want me to! Let's have a dialogue and work together to turn this around.'

The head agreed to give him one last chance. Jade and I began having Dior to stay with us every weekend, and I'd phone him at Lisa's during the week to check he was knuckling down. I thought it was going well – so I was surprised to get the call from the head a month later.

'I'm sorry, Mr Blades, but I'm going to have to expel Dior!' he said.

'Wait, what?' I gasped. 'I've been working with him. I thought that everything was OK. What happened?'

The headmaster sighed, and explained. Dior had been cheeking his class teacher again and had been sent to the head's office. Instead of going, he had stood in the middle of the playground, used a textbook to light a cigarette, and had a smoke as the book burned.

Now it was *my* turn to sigh. I didn't even try to argue Dior's case. 'I understand, and I agree with you,' I told the head. 'You can't let that go on in your school – it would be anarchy!'

So, that was that. Dior was kicked out of school. *Now what do we do?*

There was talk of sending him to a pupil referral unit for problem kids, but I didn't want to do that because I'd worked with some of those with Street Dreams and I was not a big fan. So, I arranged with Lisa that Dior would come to live with me and Jade.

When he moved in, I explained the house rules to him. Dior was used to quite a chilled regime at his mum's place, but I said he wouldn't be able to lie in bed all day at ours. He would have to get up and put a shift in, working with us on Out of the Dark.

He did, for a while. Dior rubbed along fine with me, Jade and Zola: Zola loved her new big brother. But then, after a few weeks, he decided our routine was not to his liking and went back to live with his mum again.

OK, fair enough. I found him another opportunity. In Street Dreams, we had done some work with the Peter Jones Academy, a foundation set up in Buckinghamshire by the *Dragon's Den* entrepreneur to help motivate young people to find good careers.

I spoke to my contact there. 'Will you give Dior an interview, please?' I asked. 'You don't have to give him a place, but just give him some idea of the potential he might have. Who knows? It might switch him on.'

He agreed, and Dior bowled off to Amersham one afternoon to talk to them. He hadn't even made it back to my place before the interviewer from Peter Jones called me up.

'We want to offer him a place!' he told me.

Do what? I was flabbergasted. 'But I only asked you to give him a test interview!' I said.

'I know, but he's really good!' the guy replied. 'He's smart. I think if he lets us work with him, he can achieve a lot.'

I told Dior when he got in . . . and he greeted the news with a shrug. He just wasn't interested. I offered to hire him private tutors to get him up to speed, and make up for being kicked out of school, but he still didn't want to know. He turned Peter Jones down flat.

Well, what can you do? You can't live your kids' lives for them. I was just glad to have Dior back in my life again. He's very charismatic and I knew he'd be able to charm his way into any job that he *did* want to do.

And, in time, that is what he did.

Out of the Dark was coming into its own now and it was really running us ragged. Jade and I still had little Street Dreams projects going on the side and so I was juggling furniture restoration, running youth clubs and countless meetings. It was pretty intense.

It's funny: whenever I see old photos of me from that time, I was as skinny as a whippet! We always seemed to be running between jobs and from one project to another. It was exhilarating, but exhausting.

While I was pushing myself to the max every day, I had a bit of a health scare. Having started at the ripe of old age of twelve, by now I had been a seasoned smoker for thirty years. I was a twenty-a-day man; rolls-ups, mostly. They were as much part of my life as breathing.

One morning I was sitting on my bed putting my socks on and I started to get bad chest pains. I felt like I couldn't breathe, and had to lie on the bed. I was banging my foot on the floor to get Jade's attention but it was five painful minutes before she heard me and came upstairs.

Jade dialled 999 and an ambulance quickly arrived. Three paramedics came in and said I was having all the symptoms of a heart attack. They took me down to the ambulance, plugged me into a machine and changed their minds – no, I was having an angina attack.

It passed quickly but it was a bit of a wake-up call. 'You have *got* to give up smoking!' said Jade, and I knew she was right. To show that I meant it, I went to see a guy called Ian, who hypnotized smokers to get them to give up.

I rolled up a Rizla and had a smoke outside his house, in case it was my last ever, then went through to his office, which was at the end of his garden. Ian chatted to me about giving up, and this and that, then he suddenly said, 'OK, that's it! You're sorted!'

'Eh?' I asked. 'When are you going to hypnotize me, then?'

Ian laughed. 'I've done it!' he said. 'You were asleep and snoring your head off! And now you won't want to smoke any more.'

I thought he was taking the mick. But, driving home, I realized that, for once, I didn't fancy a fag. I carried my Rizlas and tobacco around for the next two months, in case the urge returned. But it never did. I had to admit that, yep, Ian *had* hypnotized me after all.

Out of the Dark took a lot out of us. Jade and I knew

what we were doing with Street Dreams by now but, with the furniture business, I still felt like we were flying by the seat of our pants. The days had no fixed end. I'd often be sanding chairs into the early hours of the morning.

Jade had organized a committee to help us run Out of the Dark and so we had trustees to guide us and pitch in a little cash every now and then. They meant well, but they didn't always understand the principles the project was based on.

We had a little issue at one point with some of the young people not turning up for their sessions, which put us behind with production. One of our trustees had a very capitalist-minded solution.

'If they're not working quick enough, why not sack them and bring in some Polish workers?' he suggested. I had to gently explain: 'No, mate, that's not what we're about. Our business is to help young people!'

Another trustee suggested that, instead of always restoring junk-shop and second-hand furniture, we should design some chairs ourselves and knock them up quickly out of MDF.

Aaargh! Out of the Dark was all about making neglected old pieces beautiful again and restoring their faded glory. We were creating works of art and we were one hundred per cent sustainable. We wouldn't touch MDF with a bargepole!

Some of the kids got so into the furniture restoration that they wanted to pursue it as a career. I worried that it might not be possible for them. My alma mater, Buckinghamshire New University, used to have strong links with the local trade but had recently shut down all of its furniture courses.

Luckily, Ercol, one of the few original manufacturers left in the area, then came to us saying they wanted to feed more British-born youths into their apprentice programme, which was then mostly full of East Europeans. That was great – it gave our kids a possible route forward.

Street Dreams' main source of income was commissions from police and local authorities, but Out of the Dark was different. We had to generate most of our money from selling the restored furniture. It was going OK on that side, but we wanted to ramp things up.

Jade and I started going to trade fairs and trying to get appointments with big retailers such as John Lewis and Selfridges. I was proud of the work that Out of the Dark were doing and I thought our pieces *deserved* to be in places like that – plus, the moolah would help to keep us afloat.

We had a great breakthrough at a trade fair in Birmingham. Jade got talking on our stand to a buyer from Heal's, the big furniture retailer with its flagship store on Tottenham Court Road in central London. He thought our stuff was cool and said they'd like to do something with us.

Heal's were amazing with us. Because they admired the work we were doing with the kids, they let us sell our furniture in their shop and gave us all the money from any sales, without taking commission. They even donated their own broken furniture for us to do up and sell on.

It felt like a breakthrough – and then we got another stroke of luck that really pitched us into the limelight.

Jade had been talking to the *Guardian* newspaper and they told us they wanted to shoot a short video about Out of the Dark to run on their website. They asked if they could send a cameraman down to spend a few days filming me working with the young people.

Excellent! Yeah, no problem!

The video producer they sent down was a Frenchman, who turned up on the first day with . . . no camera. *Huh?* He was a cool guy, though, and Jade and I talked him through the business and what we were trying to do. He listened and seemed to take it all in.

The next morning, he arrived again still with no camera and just hung about the workshop watching us. He didn't get in the way but I was baffled – what was going on here? Had he got a hidden camera? Had I misunderstood what was going on?

The geezer wandered in on the third day with no camera again, and I had had enough. I collared him for a chat. 'Look, I don't mean no disrespect, mate,' I began. 'But I thought you were here to make a film – when do you intend to start?'

The guy's reply could not have been more confident – nor more French. 'The thing that I need to film?' he said, with a Gallic shrug. 'It has not happened yet!'

Blimey! 'OK,' I said, with a laugh. 'You're the boss!'

He did bring his equipment for the next two days and filmed me working with the kids and driving through High Wycombe telling him about the town's furniture history. It was all fairly low level, yet when I saw the guy's finished film a few days later, I was gobsmacked. Because it was fantastic.

He opened with me telling him how kids working at Out of the Dark would sometimes send me text or WhatsApp photos of furniture they'd found by the side of the road, asking if I wanted it for us to fix. I loved the fact that they were so keen.

'They're urban types, but they're collecting stuff like they're Wombles!' I laughed. I was more serious talking about how Out of the Dark was all about refurbishing furniture but, at heart, we were trying to recycle, or upcycle, the young people.

'Let's say a young person has been kicked out of school or they have behaviour problems, or whatever the case may be,' I said. 'It doesn't mean that you must give up on that person!'

The video showed me talking about a young guy called Yasser, whom I had kicked off the project for not turning up, and then asked to come back. It also spoke to Yasser, who said he'd gone off the rails because he'd never had a dad, 'but now Jay is a bit of a father figure to me'.

I felt quite emotional when he said that. The video was a brilliant advert for Out of the Dark and the *Guardian* later told Jade that thousands of people had watched it – it had gone viral. And it absolutely opened the floodgates in terms of people knowing about the venture.

Suddenly Jade was fielding scores of enquiries about Out of the Dark, and orders for the furniture, every single day. It was hard for her even to answer all the calls. In fact, one guy told us he had rung six times before he had finally got through.

His name was Gerald Bailey and it was a Sunday lunch-time when we finally picked up the phone to him. He explained to Jade that he was a businessman based in Wolverhampton who was just driving back from London – could he call in that afternoon to buy some furniture?

Sure, why not?

Jade and I met Gerald at the workshop. He was a black man, about the same age as me, and he turned up with an Asian guy named Rav. Subconsciously, my natural conditioning kicked in – *oh, the Asian geezer is in charge*! It's sad, but I just never imagined a black guy being the boss.

We walked around the workshop and Gerald was ordering a lot of stuff – 'We'll have that, and this one, and that one if you can do it in red!' – but I was addressing my answers to the Asian guy. It was a big order so I said I'd get right back to them.

I called Gerald's work number the next day and he picked up: 'Ah, yes! How are you doing, Jay?'

'Good, thanks,' I said. 'Can I speak to Rav, please?'

'Rav? Why do you want to speak to Rav?'

'To do the deal on the furniture?'

'You are doing the deal with me, Jay!' Gerald said. 'I'm the boss!'

It turned out that Gerald wasn't just the boss – he was a very big deal indeed. He was the co-founder and owner of a sixteen-store clothes chain called Diffusion, not to mention the main distributor of G-Star clothes throughout Britain. This guy was a serious player!

It blew me away because I had never before come across a black guy in such a position of power. I admired what he had achieved and so was intrigued to know more about him, and we launched into a wide-ranging chat on that telephone call.

Gerald did me a very generous deal on the furniture because he said he was impressed with Out of the Dark, and the fact Jade and I were doing things for the community for no money. He became a floating trustee on the project. We valued his advice because he knew what he was talking about.

Another side-effect of the *Guardian* film was that suddenly I had TV production companies getting in touch with me via Jade. They said they thought I might be good on TV and had various ideas and concepts for shows.

Jade would knock a lot of them back because she didn't like the sound of them. Or we would have a talk with the TV people that came to nothing. It was never a big deal and I never really expected anything to come from it: *Television? That's just not my world!*

Occasionally, they would get as far as filming a pilot for a series. A Glasgow production company called Friel Kean came to High Wycombe and did a bit of shooting for a prospective show they wanted to call *Money for Nothing*. It seemed to be about salvaging stuff from rubbish tips.

They gave me a couple of old bits of furniture and filmed me restoring them and talking about what I was doing. It was all very pleasant and easy but then they went away and, as usual, we heard nothing more. I guessed they were having trouble getting commissioned.

But I *was* suddenly to find myself on television – via a completely different route.

Our relationship with Heal's was still brilliant. They wanted to engage more with their customers, and asked if I would give a few furniture-repair workshops in their central London store. They said that we could charge for the sessions and keep the profits.

It was a no-brainer and so I started giving occasional one-day courses in the store, teaching stuff like how to reupholster chairs. It all helped to promote Out of the Dark. A cool lady called Lisa McCann came to one of the courses, and asked if she could have a word with me afterwards.

'I'm a TV producer and I do a lot of work with Kirstie Allsopp,' she told me. 'I think you'd be perfect to appear on this year's edition of *Kirstie's Handmade Christmas*. Would you be interested?'

Crikey! This was an offer that came totally from left field, but it sounded like a good opportunity to plug Out of the Dark and my first response to new things was still to give them a try: *Yeah! Why not?* Jade agreed that it sounded cool so I decided to go for it. *OK! I'm in!*

The nature of television being what it is, they were filming the show well in advance of Christmas, so a few days later I rocked up at an address in northwest London. I wasn't all that nervous: more intrigued by what this new experience might be like.

They were filming in Kirstie Allsopp's actual house and it was a right big place. Kirstie was friendly and cool, but very preoccupied by the issue of which Jimmy Choo shoes she should wear for the show. An assistant kept vanishing upstairs and coming down with yet another pair.

The show was about exactly what it said on the tin: creating handmade objects and decorations for Christmas. Kirstie and Lisa wanted me to demonstrate how to make a driftwood Christmas tree, and I spent nearly all day sitting around the kitchen before it was my turn.

It was a simple process. I whitewashed an old pallet to use as a base and nailed pieces of driftwood to it. Kirstie and her kids had scavenged the wood from the beach on their holidays. I arranged them into the distinctive pyramid shape of a Christmas tree, then fastened the whole thing to a wall.

Kirstie and I worked side by side arranging the wood as the cameras rolled. She asked me about Out of the Dark and we chatted about how to make the tree as we arranged the driftwood together. We did it all in one take, and when we had finished it looked pretty good, if I say so myself.

It was interesting to see how TV worked at first hand and I enjoyed the whole experience, but to me it was a means to an end: to promote Out of the Dark. I didn't see television as a world I would get into, or even imagine I would ever do any more. It just felt like a fun adventure.

After we finished filming, Kirstie Allsopp said a very cool thing to me. She said she loved what Out of the Dark was doing as a charity, but she knew she could never do anything like it, because she is too posh and would sound as if she was talking down to the kids. It wouldn't work.

Kirstie said that she admired us and she would support us and help to get us exposure in any way that she could. And the first way that she wanted to do this was to ask me to take part in a spin-off live event that she was involved with called The Handmade Fair.

It sounded like another valuable publicity platform, so in September 2014 we went along to the inaugural event at Hampton Court. The Handmade Fair was as genteel and well-heeled as you might expect. It was kind of like Glastonbury for arts-and-crafts people.

It was a proper big event and over three days, more than a thousand people visited the Out of the Dark stand to have a butcher's at us. Four hundred of them attended our workshops, where I taught them how to sand down furniture and the basics of reupholstery.

The festival was a cool experience and, back in High Wycombe, Jade and I felt like public property. What with Street Dreams and now Out of the Dark, we were so rooted in the local community that it felt as if everybody in the town knew us.

Some weekends, Jade would basically place me under house arrest. She knew if she sent me out to buy a loaf of bread, I'd bump into so many people who wanted advice or just to chat that I would be gone for two hours. 'You're not going out!' she'd laugh. 'Don't leave the house!'

I loved the way that our community felt like a family. It was a feeling I had not really had since I was living on the estate in Hackney as a kid. When I thought about how my life was shaping up, I realized that I should feel on top of the world.

Yet there was a dark cloud gathering over me. There was a thought in the back of my mind that I had been in total denial about, but that had now forced itself centre stage and become so dominant that it had become impossible for me to ignore.

I wasn't sure if I wanted to be with Jade any more.

We had had a lot of stress lately. Although Out of the Dark had been racing ahead, it always felt financially very hand-to-mouth. We had to depend on sales to finance everything, and we always felt one bad month away from not being able to pay the mortgage or the rent on our workshop.

We had just picked up the promise of a great contract for £50,000 to decorate a whole new office complex. We were so excited and so were the young people. We could do so much with that money – but then a new architect came in who didn't want anything to do with us.

The job got cancelled and it messed up our immediate plans for Out of the Dark quite badly. In addition, *any* couple who both live and work together will sometimes find the arrangement claustrophobic, and it was happening to us.

Jade and I would never bicker in front of Zola, but it seemed to me that our passionate discussions into the night about work, life, anything and everything had a new edge to them. A new dissatisfaction. I could see what was happening but I felt powerless to stop it.

I was falling out of love. I knew that we still loved each other, but I didn't think we were in love any more.

Jay and Jade. The dynamic duo. We had been together for fifteen years. We had achieved miracles: the power couple, always working, plotting and scheming. Yet maybe the one thing we had *not* worked at properly was our relationship.

Jade was driven, and so was I, and our drive had always been about *development*. But we had been developing our business, developing us as an entity, as a project, and we had lost sight of developing us as a couple. As two people in a marriage. As a family.

In fact, the more I looked at our relationship now, the more we didn't look like a couple at all. We looked like a business partnership. A very good business partnership, but one that was about to split up.

We didn't really talk about it. Jade is a super-smart woman and I'm sure she sensed that we were on the slide as much as I did. But her instincts were always that we

203

could mend things; problem-solve; set a goal, and hit it. Jade assumed we could *develop* our way out of our malaise.

Sadly, I didn't share her optimism. Because I sensed that we were in big, big trouble.

Jade had given me a stature in High Wycombe. She had pushed me, coaxed me, helped me formulate my dreams. She had *developed* me. Jade had been by my side every inch of the way as I had turned my life around.

How could I not love her any more?

I knew if I left it would not just be the end of me and Jade – *of me, Jade and Zola* – but also the end of Out of the Dark. The end of Street Dreams. It broke my heart even to think of letting down all the young people who trusted us and who depended on us.

I didn't want to break up everything that Jade and I had achieved over so many years. And, God help me, *I didn't want to leave Zola.* I'd always wanted to be the perfect father for her – the kind of man she would eventually want to marry.

Why the hell would she want to marry a man like me – the kind of man who would leave his wife?

I would have loved to ask somebody for advice – but who could I talk to? I was the man who supported the community. I was the Wizard of Oz; the guy who could stop young people fighting, or selling drugs, or being racist. I was the geezer who could help people and fix stuff. Who could *repair things*.

Now, it was *me* that needed help and fixing – but I felt as if there was nobody I could turn to.

For weeks, I agonized as I lay awake in bed, late at night, Jade sleeping next to me. *Was I really going to do this?* But

I knew the awful truth. I couldn't ignore it: I wasn't in love with Jade any more. It meant there was only one decision I could make.

When I told Jade that I thought we were over, she was shocked. I think she thought I might change my mind. When she realized that I wasn't going to, our reality changed. *Everything changed.*

Jade said we couldn't carry on doing Out of the Dark if we weren't a couple. She was right. We were only the dream team with both of us there: me dealing with the kids, her running the business side. That had always been our special formula. Without it, we were fucked.

Jade didn't feel able to be involved now we were splitting, so I began trying to handle the administration and finances as well. It was beyond me. I couldn't do it. We had one or two people working with us who we had to make redundant. It was a nightmare.

Jade and I were still living in the same house but in separate rooms and no longer a couple. You could cut the tension with a knife. It was hard for Zola, who was now eight – it was a lot for us *all* to cope with. There was nothing healthy about the situation.

I was feeling huge amounts of guilt. It was a mess and *it was all my fault.* I was the one who had bought the happy house, our family home, our business, all crashing down. I was the one unable to keep a loving relationship going. It was all down to me. I'd fucked up.

Well done, Jay! Here you go again!

It was too much internal pressure to cope with and I couldn't do it. I just snapped. Something in me *broke*. Late one evening in April 2015, I knew I couldn't take it any more.

I have to get out of here. Now! Or I don't know what I'll do!

It was like an out-of-body experience. It was about nine o'clock when Jade was sitting reading in the front room and I watched myself sweep past her. 'I'm going!' I said to her as I passed. She looked up, puzzled.

Going where? How? Why?

I had no idea. I went outside and I got into my loved but battered old BMW Tourer, a car that had seen many previous owners. I climbed into the car and I closed the door.

And I started to drive.

11

Driving through a tunnel of light

I HADN'T PLANNED TO LEAVE. I HADN'T PLANNED ANY-*thing*. I hadn't packed a bag, or even picked up my phone. I just got in my car and drove.

Where was I going? I had no idea.

I wasn't thinking about where I was driving. If someone had asked me, I don't think I could even have told them where I was. I just pointed the car at the road ahead of me and drove.

As it happened, I turned onto the M40. I could just as easily have gone anywhere. I drove through the dark, and into the night, and I felt as if I was driving into a tunnel. The headlights from the cars coming the other way were the walls.

I used to watch *Star Trek*, and now I felt as if I was one of the crew, going into warp factor. I felt as if I were beaming up to somewhere else, some*thing* else. I only had one mission right now: to drive.

One thought was going around and around my head: *I am a failure. A total, direct failure.* I had spent years fixing things: chairs, communities, estates, homeless people, young people. I had fixed and repaired all of those things, but now I couldn't fix my relationship.

That repair job was beyond me. I couldn't fix me.

I was a failure.

Everything came crashing down around me. I was in a cloud of dust and I couldn't see anything. And as the dust cleared, there was nothing to see. There was nothing left.

This is it! I thought. *It's over. There is no way forward. I've got nothing. Fuck-all. All those things I achieved – they've all gone now. They're worth nothing . . .*

I drove on through the tunnel of light. I had no idea how long I'd been driving for. *Minutes? Hours?* Somehow, I seemed to have pulled off the M40 and onto the M5.

I don't remember doing that.

Who cares? I've got nothing.

I'm a failure.

I might as well end it all . . .

I drove under a motorway bridge. Its concrete supports caught my eye through my tunnel of light. A half-thought formed in my brain: *I'll just crash into the next one I come to. End it all. End all of this. Why not? I've got nothing left . . .*

The next motorway bridge had a barrier around it. *Damn!* So did the one after that. And the one after that.

They all did. It didn't even occur to my numb, dumb brain that they *all* had barriers around them – maybe to stop idiots like me from doing what I wanted to do now.

I couldn't crash. I couldn't end it. I had to keep going. So, I just kept driving, and driving, and driving, lost in my tunnel of light. . .

I was in a totally dark place. I couldn't even think straight about the effect that what I was doing – *what was I doing?* – would have on my kids, who I loved more than life itself. All I knew were the thoughts swirling around and around my head . . .

I've lost everything. I've ruined everything. I'm a failure . . .

BLIP! BLIP! BLIP!

A noise, and a flashing light on the dashboard, jolted me out of my stupor. My battered old BMW was not great on fuel consumption and now a light was blinking at me like a heartbeat monitor: *BLIP! BLIP! BLIP!* It was telling me that I was nearly out of petrol.

Oh, right! I looked up to see a service station ahead and turned off the motorway. I got petrol and, as I paid in the shop, my eyes lit upon the racks of cigarettes.

I hadn't smoked since Ian had hypnotized me three years earlier. *Let's start again now! Why not?* I bought a pack, climbed back in my car and drove on. The tunnel of light consumed me again.

I was still in the out-of-body experience that had enveloped me as I walked past Jade in our front room. If anybody had asked me what I was doing, I couldn't have told them. *My only mission was to drive.*

I had no track of time in the tunnel of light. But now I was deep in the middle of the night, the lights were getting fewer and scarcer. And I was getting tired. I felt like I needed to . . . *close down.*

I went where the car took me. I didn't read the exit signs by the side of the motorway. *I don't think I could.* I pulled off at a random slip road, drove on for who-knows-how-long and came to a near-deserted car park next to some kind of retail park or mini-industrial estate.

I turned into it, and parked.

I felt like I was asleep. Whatever was happening to me was all a weird dream. I felt numb, like someone could have stabbed me and I'd have felt nothing. I didn't feel hot, or cold: I didn't feel anything at all. I felt like I was dead.

Well, I did feel one thing: *hungry.* I looked around me at the closed retail park. Argos, Homebase . . . *McDonald's!* The big yellow M. It must have been a twenty-four-hour one because the lights were on and it was open. In my dream, I saw myself walk over and order a double cheese-burger.

I sat back in my driver's seat, ate the burger and had my first smoke in four years. *I'll get some more petrol and I'll drive again,* I thought to myself. *I'll just kick this chair back and have a few minutes' rest first . . .*

BANG!

I woke up with a jolt. The sunshine was pouring through the BMW's windscreen and the car park had got proper full. Purposeful shoppers with bags were milling around. It was morning. It was a new day.

And I still felt exactly the same.

No feeling. Numb. Asleep. Dead.

I think I got out of the car and walked around the car park. I'm not sure. I must have done because, somehow, I worked out that I was in Wolverhampton. *Wolverhampton.* A city I knew nothing about, had no connection with, and had never been to before.

So what? I couldn't have cared less. It made as much sense as anywhere else.

I didn't have my phone with me and it didn't matter. *Who would want to hear from me?* I didn't want to turn around and head back to High Wycombe. *There was too much pain there. Too much failure.* I had nowhere to go, so that was what I did.

I went nowhere.

I don't know how many days I stayed in that car park. Perhaps three. Possibly four. Maybe five. I don't know what I did. Perhaps I drove around the streets, but I don't think so. I may have gone into the retail stores, but I don't remember.

I think I just sat in my car. *Doing nothing. Feeling nothing.* The extreme introvert who had taken on way, way too much, fucked it all up, and had now given up.

Given up on life. Given up on myself. Beyond repair.

Days and nights came and went in that car park. I was there but not there; present, yet absent. I was alone with my thoughts, yet I wasn't thinking of anything. I just sat, getting more and more lost in myself.

Then one morning I looked at myself in the driving mirror above the dashboard. *Wow! Man, I looked shit!* I had days of growth on my chin. My eyes were red, bloodshot, panicky. And what was that awful pen-and-ink in the car?

It was me. After days without so much as washing my hands, I didn't half stink.

Some animal instinct in me thought: *You need to get*

cleaned up, mate! I started my car engine, drove into the middle of Wolverhampton and managed to find a hotel. I looked – and smelled – like a tramp as I walked into reception.

I didn't know if they'd even give me a room. They did. I showered – and put my dirty clothes back on. They were all I had. I ordered room service and had my first real meal in days (I'd lost a stone since I fled High Wycombe).

And I lay on a proper bed and passed out.

The next morning, after breakfast, I walked aimlessly through the streets. I was still numb. Still outside of my body, watching myself go. *Still dead.*

When I walked back into the hotel, a receptionist called me over.

'There are some people here to see you, Mr Blades,' she said.

Huh? I don't know anyone in Wolverhampton! Do I?

But she was right. There were people to see me. Three of them. *And they wanted to lock me up.*

While I was in my tunnel of light and then my car park, a lot of shit had been going on. A lot of shit that I didn't know about. And a lot of people had been looking for me.

When I had walked out on Jade, without a bag or even my phone, she had been worried at the state I was in. With no way of contacting me, she had called the police. They had declared me a missing person and started a nationwide search.

It had been a proper full-on investigation. There had even been stories in the local paper:

POLICE HUNT MISSING HIGH WYCOMBE
FURNITURE RESTORER JAY BLADES

And technology had tracked me down.

In the retail park, my BMW had happened to be parked out of sight of the CCTV cameras. But when I drove into Wolverhampton, the cameras had picked me up, and numberplate-recognition technology had helped the cops to track me down to this hotel.

And now, here we were!

My visitors were a policeman, a psychiatric nurse, and . . . someone from social services? If I'm honest, I didn't know who they all were. I was still in a daze. Still numb. Nothing made sense. Including this.

'We need to ask you a few questions, sir,' the policeman said.

'Why?'

'Come with us.'

We went to a little office in the hotel and the psychiatric nurse began asking me questions off a clipboard. I answered on autopilot. The weird thing is, I don't have the slightest recollection what it was that they were asking me.

I still felt like *I wasn't really there*: it was all happening to somebody else. It was all part of my dream. But then I got jolted awake – by a remark I overheard the nurse say to the policeman.

'I'm not *sure* yet that we need to section him. . .' she murmured.

Suddenly, I was a bit livelier. A bit more engaged.

'*Sectioned*?' I asked. 'What do you mean, sectioned? Why?'

'We think you might be a danger to yourself, sir,' said the policeman.

Wow! The nurse finished her questions and my three captors went into a huddle in the corner of the room. From what I could hear, they didn't *think* I needed to be sectioned, but they weren't sure. Then there was a knock at the door. A guy that I knew walked in.

It was Gerald Bailey.

12

The *Stig of the Dump* of Wolverhampton

GERALD BAILEY, THE OWNER AND CHIEF EXECUTIVE OF Diffusion, walked into that room as if it was the most natural thing in the world for him to be there. And he immediately took charge of the situation.

'*I'll* look after this gentleman,' he told the officials. They seemed quite pleased to be rid of me and agreed to pass me into his care. He had to sign some form or other, as did I, and then we left.

As Gerald and I walked to his car, he filled in the gaps for me. When the police had called Jade to say they had found me in Wolverhampton, she had phoned the one person she knew in the city. She had asked him if he could find me and check that I was OK.

Well, Gerald was to do a *lot* more than that.

We sat in his car and Gerald started talking to me. He

was saying . . . well, to be honest, I have no idea what he was saying. Because I just burst into tears.

I sat in his plush motor and I absolutely sobbed. Proper, shoulder-heaving, gut-wrenching, inconsolable sobs. Everything poured out of me. A sea of emotion washed me away. I bawled and I howled.

I was brought up not to cry. To always act tough. I had never cried in front of another man before – certainly not in front of another *black* man! But sitting in front of Gerald Bailey, a very business-orientated guy whom, really, I hardly knew, I totally lost it. Lost all control.

It all came out. Everything that was pent up in me. It may sound weird, but I felt like a snake that was shedding its skin. I felt like I was having an electric shock, or *giving birth to myself*. I felt as vulnerable as a new-born baby.

Years later, an interviewer asked me to identify the most significant moment in my life. I said it was the day I sat in Gerald Bailey's car and cried. Because those tears brought me back to life. They ended the week-long meltdown that had consumed me.

When I stopped crying, I had got my feelings back. The numbness had passed. I was awake again. *I was alive again*.

I was alive again . . . but also, I felt awkward and self-conscious. I had just bawled my eyes out in front of this hard-headed businessman. I felt like I was sitting in front of him naked. How would he react? Would he take the piss out of me? Would he laugh?

Well, Gerald Bailey reacted to me crying my heart out in his smart leather front-passenger seat in a very shrewd and specific way. He acted as if it had never happened.

'Jay, I have a project that I want you to help me with,' he

began. 'You need something to focus on, and I know you are good at building communities. I'm going to take you to look at it now and then you can meet some people.'

Huh? I had just sobbed in front of Gerald, I was sitting there in stinking clothes I had worn for a week, I felt like I was naked, and he was . . . taking me to a business meeting?!

Now, I can see that Gerald was being super-smart. He could see the state I was in, he knew the kind of person that I am, and he sussed that the best thing would be to give me a practical project to zoom in on. At the time, I just thought he was crazy.

But I didn't say anything. Gerald drove me to a large disused warehouse conversion near the city centre. I trailed from room to room after him as he explained that he intended to transform it into a co-working space for the local creative community to come together.

Gerald explained that he wanted it to be a vibrant place where people could work in an atmosphere of creativity. Those sorts of places were springing up all over London, especially on my home turf of Hackney, but were rarer in places like Wolverhampton.

'Right, now I'll introduce you to some people you'll be working with,' he said.

Gerald drove us to the main Diffusion store in Wolverhampton. We went up to the offices, which were full of the kind of young people you would *expect* to be working in a high-end fashion store's headquarters. They all looked beautiful, glamorous and fabulously done up.

Which was more than you could say for me right now.

As Gerald introduced me and I awkwardly shook people's hands, I was painfully aware that I looked like somebody who had been sleeping in their car for a week – because I had – and my clothes stank to high heaven. I wanted to tell them all:

This is not me! I'm normally quite a dapper geezer!

It felt like it was my first day at a new school and Gerald was my big brother, walking me there and looking after me. I felt vulnerable and ashamed – *naked* – so I parked myself in the corner with a cup of tea and didn't say a lot as Gerald chaired a meeting about the project.

'Right, we're leaving!' Gerald told me when it was over. *Phew!* He took me down to the street and we stopped outside Sainsbury's.

'You don't have anything with you, do you?' he asked me. 'No.'

He handed me some money. 'OK, go in there and buy some toiletries!' Then we went to his apartment, which was a proper bachelor pad, and he gave me a towel and laid about twenty items of clothes on the bed in his spare room.

'Go and clean yourself up and put some of these on,' he instructed me. 'And then we have places to go.'

It was the weirdest day. Gerald could see I wasn't functioning properly and so he just took control. That evening he took me to his brother's house for dinner. His brother went by the rather curious name of Pie. Their uncle was also there: a pastor called the Reverend Ken Brown.

We sat and ate dinner, they all talked to me about where I was in life and where I wanted to be, and I cried again. I sobbed in front of three black guys and it felt weird but OK. I was naked again, but they gave me love. It was a powerful moment.

The next day, over breakfast in his flat, Gerald told me

that he wanted me to handle a lot of meetings with the local authorities and councillors about the warehouse project. 'I can only do business,' he told me again. '*You* do community. But you need new clothes for all of your meetings.'

Gerald sent me to the G-Star flagship store in Birmingham and told me to get whatever I wanted on his account. It was cool gear but I didn't want to take the piss, so I just got a couple of nice shirts and trousers. Which didn't impress Gerald when I got home carrying one bag.

'What's *this*?' he asked, pulling the stuff out of the bag. 'You need more than this! Go back!' He called G-Star in advance, and when I got there again, they had the whole shop laid out for me in my size. I could hardly carry all my bags home on the train.

It was unbelievable how much Gerald Bailey, a man I had only met once in my life, was now doing for me. With his help, I was beginning to feel like I was on the mend – well, it was hard to feel naked, with as many clothes as that! I was beginning to see a way to make it out of my dark place.

And I phoned Jade.

Our first chats after I had had my breakdown were painful. Jade was worried about me, and for me, but she was also angry with me and she didn't hold back from telling me. She was upset, confused and wanted to know what the fuck was going on.

I couldn't tell her because I still didn't know. But I knew we were over and we needed to get a divorce. I felt guilty as hell, though, and I let her use me as a verbal punchbag when we spoke. And I felt like I deserved it.

I told Jade that I thought it would take me a year to get back on my feet but, once I had, I would make sure that she and Zola never wanted for anything. I'd make everything up to her. It didn't stop her being mad with me – but she knew I am a man of my word. She believed me.

A lot of people had been very worried about me when I vanished and I had to make a few trips to show them that I was OK. We could speak on the phone but they needed to see me face-to-face to be fully reassured. I went to Luton to see Maria and Levi, and Oxford to see Dior.

I also went back to High Wycombe to see Zola and Jade. It was hard but it was always going to be. My disappearance had been a big news story in the town and the local paper did a spread on me when I was found safe.

While I was there, I bumped into one of the young guys that we had worked with via Street Dreams. He now worked in marketing and he had been following my recent antics *very* closely.

'Jay, when you was on the run, you was *well* famous!' he said. 'You should've made an album! You'd be rich, man!'

'But I can't sing!' I said.

He shrugged. 'So what? *Loads* of guys who make albums can't sing. It's all about exposure – and you had *plenty*!"

Back in Wolverhampton, we got to work. Gerald fixed me up meetings with the local bodies involved in the warehouse project: the council, housing associations, the local university. He also set me up with a sidekick as I found my feet.

Christine was a senior buyer of the women's lines at Diffusion and was very well connected in the

Wolverhampton community. Gerald said she could open up doors for me, and he was right. Christine was invaluable as I learned the ropes.

She and I started assessing the project, working on reports and having meeting after meeting as we tried to get the project off the ground. It was interesting – but in truth it was not as interesting to me as another avenue that Gerald opened up.

He gave me my own big room in the warehouse building. 'Go in there and muck around with your arty-farty stuff!' he told me, laughing. 'Throw some paint around, or whatever it is that you do!' I took him up on the offer and started getting hold of some second-hand furniture to restore.

I was getting back to things that I knew, and life was even starting to feel slightly normal again, but then came another change. Gerald was a bit of a player with the ladies, and after I'd been crashing in his spare room for a month, he let me know that I was cramping his style.

'Jay, man, I love you, but you're in the way!' he told me, bluntly. 'I've got to concentrate on my business *and* I haven't been with a woman in a month, either! I'm sorry, my friend, but you have to go!'

But Gerald wasn't kicking me on to the streets. He did something a million times better. He sent me to live with his mum and his step-dad.

Thelma and Cass lived in a big old farmhouse near to Wolverhampton. They had a granny flat by their house and they installed me in there. And these two special people helped bring me back to life and kickstart my repair job after my breakdown. They were my life-savers.

They were a lovely old *Windrush*-era Jamaican couple.

Cass had worked as a labourer and Thelma had been a nurse. They totally looked after me. They were like having a mother, grandmother and the father that I never had all rolled into one.

Thelma was kind and loving, and Cass was an old-school Jamaican man who liked to play his dominos and drink his rum. He taught me to cook ackee and saltfish, callaloo and yam and dumplings. The two of them did so much for me. I still choke up just thinking about it.

They embraced me and took me into their home. I call my time with them my rebirth, because that was where I began to get repaired and rebuilt after I had fallen to pieces. I began to feel human again.

The three of us became a family unit. I would drive them to see their friends at the local community centre, and Thelma and Cass would proudly parade me around as 'our son from London'. It is impossible to exaggerate just how much that meant to me.

In fact, Cass was the first man – the only man – that I have ever called 'Dad'. I was sitting playing dominos with him one day, over rice and peas, and I got the sudden overwhelming urge to say something to him.

'Cass, I have *so* much love and respect for you and Thelma,' I told him. 'I would like to call you "Dad", but I don't know if I should – I don't want to show disrespect to your own children.'

Cass looked at me, and smiled. 'I would love that,' he said. He and I had such a deep, deep connection. We still do.

Zola started coming up to stay with me every three or four weeks. It was lovely to see her. It was all a big adventure for her – and Thelma and Cass instantly became a pair of loving surrogate grandparents.

Gerald said that I needed counselling after my breakdown so I started seeing somebody in Wolverhampton. She was a nice woman, and she arranged to see me for a bargain rate, because she knew that I didn't have much money.

She was good, and talking to her helped, but it wasn't professional counselling that healed me and helped to start my repair job. It was living with Thelma and Cass, and being taken into the core of their lives. I can say, with sincerity: without them, I don't think I'd be here today.

As I settled in with them, I also got to know my new home city – and I liked what I saw. Wolverhampton reminded me a lot of London in the seventies. The black community are very tight and supportive, and Thelma and Cass helped me to get accepted by them and to fit in.

I had no history at all in Wolverhampton but the people that I met, of all colours, were nice and friendly and welcoming. They had no side to them and I loved that. I sometimes say nowadays that Wolverhampton folk are the best in the country, and I'm not joking. *I mean it.*

I even got used to the accent! It's very different from London, and when I first moved there, one guy said, 'Yow'll lose your accent and talk like us soon, pal! Yow'll be a Brummie, or a yam-yam!' I laughed: 'No, I won't, mate! I don't think so!' And I haven't. *So far*, anyway . . .

The meetings for Gerald's warehouse venture were rolling on and I was intrigued by my colleague on the project, Christine. She was a classy, funny woman of around my age who was smart and carried herself with real dignity. I started looking forward to our meetings.

The project was moving forward very slowly, and in truth I was more interested in what Gerald had kindly called my 'arty-farty stuff'. I was using the space he had given me in the warehouse to get right into furniture restoration again.

I started touring Wolverhampton's second-hand shops. . . and I couldn't believe some of the bargains I was picking up! A lot of people just didn't realize the value of their old stuff. They would offload it to the local junkshop who would sell it on for a pittance.

There is a lot of wealth in Wolverhampton and people in some areas would hold garage sales to dispose of their unwanted furniture. I went to one and picked up a classic G-Plan chair for £40. I knew if I did it up and gave it a cool twist, I would sell it for ten times that.

I started going to backstreet auction houses throughout the Midlands. They had some amazing bargains. I went to one in Wolverhampton and my eyes were on stalks at one lot in the catalogue.

It was an actual Robin Day chair.

I knew enough about the history of furniture by now to know that Robin Day was one of the most important English designers of all time, and there in front of me was a genuine original! It was up for auction together with a couple of tatty old, cheap bedside cabinets.

I didn't have much money, but I knew: *I have to have that chair!* I waited impatiently for the lot to come around. And, when it did, I couldn't believe my ears.

'Do I hear an opening bid of £4.50?' asked the auctioneer.

£4.50?! I stuck my hand as high in the air as it would go.

'£5?' asked the auctioneer. A middle-aged lady on the

other side of the room put her hand up. *Damn! Was she a dealer?*

'£5.50?' I was waving at the geezer again.

'£6?' My rival was back in the lead.

Shit! I knew I couldn't compete if she had serious money, but I bid again at £6.50. At which point the woman looked over at me, pursed her lips, shook her head as if it was an astronomical sum, and dropped out. *Yes!*

I couldn't believe it! I had got a Robin Day chair for £6.50! As I waited to collect it afterwards, I got talking to my vanquished competitor. 'I was only bidding for the bedside cabinets, duck,' she admitted.

'*Really?*' I laughed. 'I'll give you the cabinets as a present, love! For nothing! Because I've got myself a £400 chair!' I can still picture her astounded face.

As the dirt-cheap furniture piled up in my warehouse space and I began restoring it and selling it on, I formalized it into a business. I called it Jay & Co. I didn't really have a vision for it in terms of a business plan. I *did* have a vision for it in terms of the designs that I wanted to create.

I wanted to move in different directions and to experiment. When I bought classic old furniture that people no longer needed, I wanted to restore it in a way that paid homage to the master craftsmen who had designed it but also to give it a new, modern twist. That mix of tradition and modernity excited me.

I would buy a beautiful chair that was no longer wanted because it was tatty and brown, or it looked old, and I'd give it a new lease of life. I'd reupholster it and paint it a certain, inventive way. I might only paint one leg – in fact, painting one leg became a bit of a minor trademark for me!

It was all about innovation, sure, but at heart it was also about history, and heritage, and preserving those qualities. I set to work in Gerald's warehouse and hoped that enough opportunities would come along to help me make Jay & Co a success.

And, as it happened, a major opportunity came along very, very quickly.

Friel Kean, the production company that had filmed the pilot for *Money for Nothing* back in High Wycombe, got back in touch with me via social media. After a couple of years of trying, they had got a commission to make the series – from the BBC. Could we meet and have a chat?

I went to see them at their office in Glasgow. The basic concept of the show was the same as I remembered from the pilot. A presenter would go to a recycling centre, salvage an item that was about to be thrown away and set about giving it some value again.

The presenter would give an old chair or table to a restorer like me to weave his magic on. The producers would then sell the restored item – and any profit made would be handed to the original person who had taken the item to the tip. Would I be interested?

Yeah! Why not?

So, every week or so, *Money for Nothing* presenter Sarah Moore would turn up in Wolverhampton with a camera crew. They'd give me an item from the recycling site – normally a chair, or an old table – and I'd fix it up for them.

It was easy and I liked doing it. My brain is wired the right way for stuff like that. I'd let my imagination run riot. I'd often find the solution for how to restore something simply by looking at the problem – and the item – from another angle.

I might turn a chair upside-down and it would give me a whole new perspective on what I could do with it. Or I would take a drawer out of a chest of drawers, fix a handle to it, turn it over and – *hey presto!* A sandwich cover! The trick was to think outside of the box.

I've heard a theory that dyslexic people have a different take on spatial awareness, which helps us to think laterally in that way. Is it true? I've no idea! I never sketch things out, I just work through gut instinct: *Oh, THAT would look good with THAT!* And it normally does.

Sarah and her team would turn up again a few days later, compliment me on what I'd done and take the item off to try to flog it. It was a fun thing to do, the money came in handy, and it helped to bring a lot more attention to Jay & Co.

This was a mixed blessing. The publicity was cool but, from the start, I was very careful to keep Jay & Co and *Money for Nothing* separate. I was making furniture I loved and I thought had real value in Jay & Co, and I made sure to keep it apart from the TV show.

Why? It was all about branding. Most exclusive designer brands are not on daytime TV and that was what I wanted Jay & Co to be. So, although I loved doing *Money for Nothing*, I kept a clear distinction between the two entities.

I was still working on Gerald's warehouse project. Christine and I were talking to the council to work out what their role in the venture would be, and to the university to see how many students they would send us. But then the rug got pulled from beneath us.

The project was dependent on us getting money from the European Social Fund, and after the Brexit vote of June 2016, that funding would no longer be available in the UK. After all of our work, it put the kibosh on the whole venture. It was a real shame.

But I still took something – or, rather, *somebody* – very important away from the project.

Over the weeks, I'd been getting closer and closer to Christine. She was a very glamorous lady and I loved her innate sense of style. As you'd expect from a fashion buyer, she knew exactly what clothes worked for her and was always beautifully dressed. She looked a million dollars.

It wasn't just her looks: we got on super-well. I could feel my interest in Christine moving beyond the professional and I wondered if she might feel the same. Thankfully, by now I had moved on from clumsily telling women 'You will be mine!' I took a rather more grown-up approach the evening that I phoned her up.

'I'd like to take you out on a date,' I said, nervously.

We went to a pub for dinner and had a lovely evening. She told me that she had two grown-up children: her son had left home, and her twenty-year-old daughter still lived with her. After that, drinks or dinner after work became a regular event for us.

Things were going well. I was loving my home life with Thelma and Cass, and Jay & Co was slowly but surely picking up steam. I had restored stuff for two series of *Money for Nothing* in quick succession and was waiting for the third to get underway when I got a call from Friel Kean.

Would I go up to Glasgow for a meeting?

When I flew up to Scotland, I met with Michelle Friel

and Jules Kean and they told me that they wanted to promote me from restoring the items to actually presenting the show. *Wow, OK!* It was a major upgrade, but I agreed to do it.

It was flattering, and I think of Michelle and Jules, like David McWhirter, as real fairy godmothers in my life – people who took a chance on me when a lot wouldn't have, and who helped me to develop. On the flight home, I felt excited and fired up.

Becoming a presenter obviously meant a huge increase in my *Money for Nothing* workload. Because, suddenly, I was the guy hanging around the council recycling sites trying to find treasure in the trash. I had to grab the jewels in the dirt before they hit the skip.

It was time to become *Stig of the Dump.*

It was an interesting process. I said in one early show that I felt like a hawk looking for prey and that was about the size of it. And it could be anything and everything. I never knew what I was looking for until I found it.

When I did spot something valuable – *is that a Chesterfield sofa?! An Ercol chair?!* – I would be over like a shot. And I took to my new role for the same reason I had done OK at Cyrenians, and got results at Street Dreams: because I have a decent knack at talking to people.

I'd wander over to the person dumping the gear and introduce myself: 'Hello, I'm Jay! What you got here, then?' They'd tell me a bit about the item and I'd ask if I could have it. They'd never say no: why would they? They were on the verge of chucking it away!

I found talking to the public, and the camera, pretty easy. A producer told me early on to talk to the camera as if it were a person, and that advice really stuck with me. It still does. Whenever I talk to a camera, I imagine I'm talking directly to the person watching it.

The new role suited me better than doing something scripted – with my dyslexia, learning a script would be a nightmare! In fact, the only thing I didn't like about it was if a director tried to put words in my mouth.

On an early *Money for Nothing* shoot, the director told me to say, 'It's an original reproduction.' *Huh? I wasn't having that!* 'It doesn't make sense, mate!' I said. 'A reproduction is a copy. It's not an original! I'm not saying it!' He and I fell out over that. But I stood my ground.

The days on the dumps could be a real slog. They didn't always run as smoothly as they looked on the screens. I'd see some characters pull up at the tip, clock our TV cameras and drive off fast. God only knows what dodgy stuff *they* were planning on dumping!

A few people didn't want to talk and just told me to piss off. I could be at a recycle site for days because it was raining and there was nobody there, or everybody was chucking away rubbish that was no use to us. Some dumps really whiffed. This was *not* the glamorous side of TV!

Yet it was worth it whenever I found a diamond in the rough – an exquisite old sideboard, or a battered but beautiful antique chair. I'd snaffle my finding and head off with it to one of our expert restorers.

The experts are what make *Money for Nothing*. They are a dream team of dedicated craftsmen and I take my hat off to them. In fact, I do that literally – whenever one of them performs an absolute miracle, I doff my cap to them. It's my sign of complete respect.

I loved meeting those guys. The first time I met Bruce Kenneth, our artisan American woodworker relocated to Yorkshire, I didn't twig at first that there was anything unusual about him. I was boggling at his amazing huge woodworking machines, and I went to shake his hand.

And then I looked again.

'You only have one arm!' I gasped. 'How do you *work* all this stuff?'

The answer is: he works it brilliantly. I remember we took Bruce bits of random wood and he carved a jaw-dropping coat stand from them. He also crafted gorgeous hammers from old waste timber. They were so beautiful that you'd never want to use them. The guy is a genius.

One week I salvaged a few sheets of scrap metal that some bloke had left over from a building job and took them up to Edinburgh to sculptor Kev Paxman. I almost felt guilty for dumping them on him. 'Good luck with that!' I told him as I left.

When I went back, Kev had melted them down and sculpted them into an intricate bird feeder, complete with little trees, leaves and acorns. It was a proper work of art. Another week, he turned a crappy old glass lampshade into one so beautiful that it took my breath away.

I gave Leigh-Anne Treadwell from the Bristol Upholstery Collective the shittiest, most basic old Argos chair you can imagine. She stripped it down to its skeleton and transformed it into a marvel that looked like a design icon. I had my hat off for the whole of that interview!

Money for Nothing gets called an 'upcycling' show but I am wary of that phrase. It doesn't pay enough homage to the master craftsmen we have working for us. They are drawing on decades of history and heritage in their work. For me, calling them 'upcyclers' cheapens them.

They are *a lot* more than that.

I quickly found that presenting *Money for Nothing* was exhausting. The filming schedule was ridiculously demanding:

1) Spend hours – or days – at a tip panning for gold;
2) Drive around the country delivering the items to the artisans;
3) Go back to them all a week later to admire their handiwork;
4) Once we'd sold the item, find the person who had taken it to the dump to give them their dosh.

It was time-consuming but I got used to the long hours and it was all worth it every time our experts turned yet another knackered old sow's ear into a gorgeous silk purse. And the show did well. Soon, it was picking up two million viewers per week. *Not bad!*

Obviously, becoming the show's presenter also meant I got paid more, and I started being able to send more moolah to Jade each month to help to look after Zola. It had worked out exactly like I had told her. It had taken a year, but I was firmly back on my feet.

I started getting recognized in the street a bit in Wolverhampton and *Money for Nothing* certainly increased awareness of Jay & Co. In fact, I had to employ a couple of people to source the furniture for me, because as soon as I walked in the door of a junk shop, their prices went right up!

My friendship with Christine was a slow burner but it was growing in its intimacy and intensity. We still weren't *quite* a couple, but when she went down to London on her Diffusion buying trips, she'd call in on me at Thelma and Cass's place on the way home.

In fact, I have a very precise memory of the second I realized that we were heading for a full-on relationship. Christine dropped in one evening while Cass was cooking. She grabbed an apron off Thelma and started to help him chop and prepare the food.

It was a small thing but it was so *natural*, and she fitted in to the family so well, that I was getting flashbacks to being a teenager and Maria coming around our house and being accepted by Mum. I felt delighted.

A-ha! I thought to myself. *Here we go! This is what I wanted!*

I'd never met Christine's kids because we had an unspoken thing that I wouldn't do that unless she and I were serious about each other. Then, one day, Christine turned up at my workshop late in the morning.

'Let's grab some lunch,' she suggested.

'OK, cool!' I agreed.

As we neared the pub, she dropped a casual bombshell: 'Oh, we're meeting my daughter here.'

What?! I was horrified! 'But I'm in my filthy workshop gear! Why didn't you tell me? I don't want to meet her like this!'

'Don't worry about it! They're waiting for us.'

They?!

I felt so nervous! When we got in and sat down, Christine's daughter was with a close friend of hers. She was lovely but fairly quiet, but for the next hour, her friend absolutely grilled me. I guess she must have been acting on instructions, but the questions were relentless:

Who are you? What do you do? Where do you live? Have you been married? Who to? Do you have children? Do you have siblings? Do you drive? Do you . . .

It went on and on, but the atmosphere stayed very friendly so I guess I must have passed whatever the test was. And, in any case, some of the information I gave her was about to change.

Thelma and Cass had helped to heal me. I was a very different, stronger man now than the wreck who had turned up on their doorstep fresh from a breakdown. I had had an amazing time living with my surrogate parents, but now I was part-repaired and it was time to move on and stand on my own two feet again.

To celebrate, I went on holiday to Tenerife shortly afterwards with Christine and her daughter. It was the first time I'd been on an all-inclusive trip, with all the food and drink paid for in advance, and I couldn't believe everything was now free. I filled my boots. I was eating about six meals a day!

While we were away, I was thinking about Jay & Co. I had had some ideas about what I wanted to do with the business – and one person in particular had inspired me.

I don't watch a lot of telly, but a documentary about Jamie Oliver had blown me away. I had admired his whole campaign to get junk food out of school dinners, and now he was launching a scheme to help young people get into the catering industry.

I wanted to do a similar thing with Jay & Co that I did with Out of the Dark. I wanted to teach young people to revamp and restore old furniture in a way that was totally sustainable. And I realized that, like Jamie, having a profile on TV would help me to support kids like that.

Which was just as well. Because my profile was just about to get a whole lot bigger.

I got asked to appear on a programme with Gok Wan for Kirstie Allsopp's production company. It was called *Fill Your House for Free* and we went around people's houses giving them upcycling (that word again!) tips and helping them to decorate their homes.

Gok was cool, full-on and full of flirty banter, and the show was a lot of fun to do. While we were filming, I met his agent, Carol Hayes. I had never had an agent but I was starting to suspect that I probably should. She seemed nice, so I asked her if she would represent me.

Carol took my number then phoned me a day or two later and said that she'd love to be my agent. And, a few days after that, she called me again – with some very interesting news.

'A production company called Ricochet have been in touch,' she said. 'Would you like to be involved in a new show called *The Repair Shop*?'

13

One big happy family

Quite a few TV production companies had got in touch with me in the wake of *Money for Nothing*. The process normally followed the same pattern. They'd tell me their idea for a show that was a dead-cert, sure-fire hit. I'd listen and say, *Yeah, sounds OK!*

Then they would go away, and it wouldn't happen.

I was used to it . . . and also, although I was on television by now, I still didn't know a lot about how it worked. The last time I had watched telly a lot was in the eighties so, to me, TV still meant *CHiPs* and *The A-Team*! The shows I loved had had car chases in, not geezers fixing furniture!

I went for a meeting with Ricochet in London and they showed me their treatment for *The Repair Shop*. It was an A4 document with a picture on the front of me and two guys I didn't know: Dominic Chinea and Will Kirk. I was at the front, I guess because I'd done the most TV.

I flicked through the treatment as they talked to me but I didn't read it. *I couldn't.* Reading still wasn't my strong suit. I listened as Emma Walsh and Sam Wilson from the company talked me through the basic concept.

And it was very basic. Ordinary people would bring treasured items into a repair shop and a team of repairers would fix them. Ordinary people; ordinary items; ordinary repairers. There wouldn't be many car chases!

The creative director of Ricochet, Katy Thorogood, had had the initial brainwave for the show. After her mother passed away, she had taken the old armchair that her mum used to sit in when she watched TV to a professional upholsterer to be refurbished.

The upholsterer had done a blinding job, and when Katy had gone to collect it, she had been so overcome by emotion that she had burst into tears. And that was the precise moment that she had the idea for *The Repair Shop*.

I can't be unique! Katy had thought. *There must be millions of people like me who would be incredibly moved to see treasured household items, and family heirlooms, restored to their former glory!*

It's true what they say . . . sometimes, the simplest ideas are the best.

I listened to Emma and Sam as they talked me through the idea for the show, and I wondered if anybody would watch something as low key as that. But I didn't say anything. These people knew *way* more about TV than me. If they thought there was a chance that the show could work, well, that was good enough for me!

After my meeting, I went downstairs and saw a guy sitting waiting to go up. I recognized him from the pictures on the front of *The Repair Shop* leaflet, so I introduced myself and shook his hand.

'Hello, mate, my name's Jay! I see we might be working together!'

'Hello, I'm Dom!' said Dom Chinea. We chatted for a minute and I left.

Ricochet wanted to film a pilot, and they called me the next week. They asked me if Jay & Co had any customers who had given me an old chair that used to belong to a relative to restore.

'Yeah, we get those all the time!' I said. 'I've got a lady coming in next week to collect one.'

'That's great!' they said. 'Can we come and film it?'

'Sure, if she doesn't mind!'

One of the Richochet creative team, Claire Egerton-Jones, turned up at Jay & Co the following week with a camera crew and filmed my customer picking up her item. Just like Katy, the lady's mum had recently died and she couldn't bear to throw her favourite armchair away.

Ricochet got exactly what they were looking for. They got their money shot. Because the second the lady saw the chair, she started crying – just like Katy had.

'Oh, Jay, this is so much better than I expected!' she said, through her tears. 'I feel like Mum is sitting here now! Thank you so much!'

From my point of view everything on *The Repair Shop* happened very quickly, and I bowled along to the workshop at the Weald & Downland Living Museum near Chichester in Sussex to film the first series. I got introduced to a lot of people in rapid succession.

I saw Dom again, and he told me he was a metalworker.

I met Will, the other guy from the front of the leaflet, who was a carpenter, and Steve Fletcher, who said he mended clocks. Kirsten Ramsay, who conserved pottery, was there, as was Lucia Scalisi, a painting conservator.

There were two toy restorers called Amanda Middleditch and Julie Tatchell, whom I immediately came to think of as The Teddy-Bear Ladies. And as I set up my tools at a repair bench in the corner of the workshop, something dawned on me: *This is going to be special.*

It was a lovely situation. We were all worker bees, which is what I call anybody who makes something, but we normally worked alone – us upholsterers, and woodworkers, and leatherworkers. We weren't usually all together in a hive, buzzing off each other.

This could be really interesting!

The first person who ever walked through the door on *The Repair Shop* was a lady called Jane, who brought in a clock that had been made by her father, Geoffrey, who was blind. I was absolutely flabbergasted.

'I've got both eyes and I can just about make a cup of tea!' I told her. 'Your dad was blind, and *he made a clock*?!' Steve did a proper good job on fixing it. Jane was very moved when she saw his handiwork.

I was originally set up in the corner where Will's bench is now, and my first customer was a woman called Helen, whose piano stool had been damaged by her dog. She was a lovely, bubbly lady – and she had clearly seen me on *Money for Nothing*.

'Jay, don't go painting one of the legs pink!' she laughed. 'I know that's your thing, but I don't want it! I just want the stool back to normal.'

Will restored the woodwork and I reupholstered the fabric parts. It looked pukka. When she came back in, we lifted off the sheet and did the big reveal. Helen has her own special place in *Repair Shop* history because she was the first person to cry on the show. She burst into tears of joy.

It was the moment the penny dropped for me. *Wow, this show is going to be even more powerful than I thought! Because it is drawing real emotion out of people!*

You might expect the transaction to be a straightforward one: 'Can you fix this for me?' 'Yeah, sure! Here it is, fixed!' 'Cheers, thanks a lot! See you later!' *But it wasn't like that.* The repairs, and the restored items, were triggering a million memories in people's minds.

They were giving them back flashes of a life, and of loved ones, that they no longer had. And it was profound.

In that first series, I was just one of the worker bees: the upholsterer in the team. I restored three or four chairs for grateful visitors to the Shop. But the producers had a lot of other jobs for me as well.

I've always been a banter merchant and the directors would ask me to go from bench to bench, chatting to the other restorers and asking how they were getting on with their work. I'd ask them questions and they'd tell me – and the cameras – what they were doing.

I liked doing it, but it took up so much time that I wasn't able to do my own repairs. One week I had a chair to fix, the lady was coming in the next morning to collect it, and I'd been so busy filming other bits that I hadn't even started it the evening before!

That day finished with all the restorers still in the workshop at ten at night, clustered around my bench helping me to do my repair. And it dawned on the producers: *If we want Jay to be our front man, he can't be a worker bee as well.*

So, the same thing happened as on *Money for Nothing.* I stopped being a restorer and became the presenter.

I was fine with this switch. It suited my personality. I've always enjoyed talking to people, and I knew from *Money for Nothing* that I am quite good at chatting to them on camera as if the camera's not there. It just becomes a fly on the wall.

The other *Repair Shop* experts are geniuses at doing repairs but they can sometimes start mentally dissecting the problem as soon as the item is handed to them. They'll look at it, thinking *Hm, I'll take the back off first!* even as the guy who gave it to them is still talking. They get distracted from listening.

It became my job to focus fully on the visitor, connect with them and get their story. *Who did this belong to? Wow, to your grandad? Great, what was his name? And what did he do?* I sought the human-interest stories that make the repairs, and the show, work.

Some of the items were a hundred years old, or more, and I wanted to give them, and their history, the respect they deserved. Because when you knew the story, you connected to the item so much more. It made you so much more invested in the repair.

I had to put our guests at their ease. I knew that when they walked in the door, they knew our faces and how many people were watching on TV, and often they were nervous. I had to relax them so they could share their story with us.

In the same way as I never read the kids' reports at Youth at Risk, I realized that I preferred not knowing the stories behind the items beforehand. I don't want to be prepped. I want to hear them for the first time at the same time as the viewers, and to react naturally.

And we heard some heart-wrenching, humbling stories. A guy called Andrew came in with a bargeware teapot for Kirsten to fix. The teapot had belonged to his wife, Jane. She had died and he had passed it down as a family heirloom to their daughter, Alice.

Alice had her own child, Lily, but then tragically died of lymphoma. And, just two months later, here was Andrew, having lost both his wife and daughter, getting the teapot repaired to eventually pass it on to his tiny granddaughter.

It was so moving and Andrew was so brave. Kirsten did a wonderful job on the teapot and then the grandad came back in with his son-in-law, Nick, holding Lily, to pick it up. I still choke up when I think about it.

I had one thought: *That's what a dad should be like!*

It struck me as an important function of *The Repair Shop: it is a place where men can cry.* Where can men show emotion, normally? Down the pub? At a football match? That's just bravado. *The Repair Shop* is one place they can let it all spill out.

It's not just the customers, either! In my time on the show, I've seen Dom cry, and Will, and Steve. I've seen Brenton get emotional. I'm not ashamed to say I've shed a few tears as well. It's natural and it's very healthy.

I always listen closely and make a lot of eye contact when people bring items into the Shop – but I soon realized that not all of our visitors were doing the same thing back! They would come in determined not to cry on the telly, and it would make them wary of me.

They'd seen me on TV and thought, *I've got to be careful with Jay – if I look at him, he'll set me off crying!* So, they would look away or stare down at the floor as they talked to me. I understood, and I was cool with it. It was entirely up to them.

One item that had me close to tears was a big old pump organ that Angie and Carmen, two sisters from Birmingham, brought in. Their mum had brought it with her when she came over from Jamaica on the *Windrush. Wow! Imagine transporting that lovely beast for weeks on that crowded ship!*

When the sisters walked in, they looked like my aunties from Hackney and I wanted to hug them. So, I did. Our organ restorer, David Burville, fixed it up good and proper, and when they came back for the reveal, all four of us were blinking back tears. It was beautiful.

It made me realize: *These aren't just items that we're fixing. They're family members! There is so much history and memories bound up in them. We're restoring family members and returning them to where they belong – the heart of the family.*

I'm not ashamed of crying, but I try to hold it together on *The Repair Shop* so I can keep the conversation flowing. But it's not always easy. It certainly wasn't when a lady called Steph came in in a wheelchair with a battered old teddy, Fred, she'd had since being born with spina bifida.

Steph had never been able to walk, and Fred had been with her for her entire life, in every hospital and for every operation. If doctors operated on her left leg, the nurses bandaged the bear's left leg up as well. The teddy-bear ladies made him look like new again. Wonderful!

Steph has since been in touch to say that Fred always sits with her to watch the show, and last time she went into hospital, all of the doctors and nurses wanted photos with him! It's a lovely story, and the essence of what *The Repair Shop* is about.

I was also really moved when Helen Bannan visited us. Helen was a former kickboxing world champion who had had to give up the sport due to slipped discs and sciatica. Her world-champion trophy, her pride and joy, had got badly burned in a house fire.

Helen's story hit me hard and we connected so well when she came in. Kirsten did a blinding job on the trophy, and I was gutted that I missed Helen coming in for the reveal because I was away filming for *Money for Nothing* that day. It upset me. I really wanted to be there.

One of our best-known repairs was when a lovely old guy called Geoff from Sunderland came in with a jukebox. Not just *any* old jukebox. When Geoff married his wife, Marie, in 1978, they had no money for a reception.

The happy couple had instead taken their wedding guests back to their house for a sandwich and a bop to the jukebox. Their first dance was to 'Moonlight Serenade' by Glenn Miller. 'I didn't expect it, but magic happened,' Geoff told me. 'Everything came together in that moment'.

Geoff talked lovingly about Maria, fighting back tears as he explained that she had died seven years earlier from a brain tumour. He found it too painful to listen to the jukebox for years. Now, he wanted to try again, but it was broken. His priceless memories were trapped inside.

When Geoff returned to find our audio expert, Mark Stuckey, had got the jukebox working like new, he dissolved into tears as he listened to 'Moonlight Serenade' again. 'It's a lovely tune,' he said, bravely. *There we were again: men, crying and expressing positive emotion.*

When they later featured Geoff and his jukebox on *Gogglebox*, all of the people sitting watching TV at home on their sofas were blubbing. I wasn't surprised. Because so was I.

One reason *The Repair Shop* works so well is that the majority of us experts are middle-aged. We've all been around the clock a few times and we've gone through life's many ups and downs. It lends us empathy.

We've often had the exact same life experiences and hard times as our guests. It means items can touch the rawest of nerves. Suzie Fletcher is our in-house leather-worker and the sister of our clock repairer, Steve. Suzie sadly lost her husband to cancer in 2013.

A lady called Julie came in with a battered old wooden horse for us to repair. Julie's husband, Paul, had tried to restore the horse back in 1987 but had also since died of cancer. Julie said she thought he had signed his name on the wood beneath the saddle.

Will took on the job, but also showed the horse to Suzie, asking if she could do something with the leatherwork. When Suzie chiselled off the saddle to find Paul's name carved underneath, it was too much for her. She burst into tears. Steve ran over to comfort his little sis.

It was incredibly moving – and this is where *The Repair Shop*'s editors come into their own. They do a blinding job of capturing the emotions while never making the scenes mawkish or exploitative. They walk a fine line and they do it with perfect balance.

I also love how *The Repair Shop* is an antidote to throw-away culture. It's all about make-do-and-mend, and recycling, and valuing the planet. If somebody has made something that's built to last, why throw it away? Why not reinvent it, lend it some TLC and give it a new life?

If we give up on old things, we're giving up on the old-timers who made them. That's a sin. As a kid, I used to love to watch Bagpuss in his shop, mending kids' broken toys. Now, I tell people of my age that *The Repair Shop* is the grown-up version of *Bagpuss*. They get it straight away.

People compare *The Repair Shop* to *Antiques Roadshow*. I see why, and they attract a similar audience. Both are proper family shows, that you can sit and watch with your grandparents *and* your children. And yet there is an important difference.

Antiques Roadshow is people wanting to flog their old items to make money. That's fair enough, but as soon as you start talking about cash, *it cheapens the item*. It makes everything more mercenary. *The Repair Shop* is never about money. It's about love, and memories, and family.

The great thing is that *The Repair Shop* team have grown into a family. We've been working together for four years now, sometimes six days per week, so we see a lot *more* of each other than some families! And we have an absolute riot. It's brilliant.

Every family has its miserable members, and Steve can be a bit on the grumpy side sometimes, but he comes alive when he gets a great job to work on. Dom is the fit, hale-and-hearty big brother who always wants to be outdoors. He takes his items outside to work on a lot of the time.

I go out to see him, shiver, and shake my head: 'Dom, man, why are you working out here? It's freezing!'

'I'm fine, Jay,' he tells me. 'I just keep moving.'

Will is our lovable little brother. He's a sensitive soul and very, very creative. Kirsten is the workshop queen: the family matriarch. If we lads are enjoying some banter and getting a bit boisterous, she'll give us a friendly-but-firm look. It says: *OK, let's calm down now, shall we?*

It's a lot gentler than a Ridley Road Look – but it has the same effect!

Suzie works with a hard material, leather, but she's one of the softest souls you could meet, a real gem. Lucia is the crazy cousin. She restores priceless paintings – but in her time off, she is out there doing street art! I look at her work and it boggles my mind. She's super-talented.

It's a genuine joy to work in *The Repair Shop*. A while back, a magazine editor came down with a photographer to do a feature on us. I think maybe she imagined the camaraderie was all put on for the cameras and she'd find us all apart and doing our own thing.

Well, she was wrong. At the end of the day, she laughed and said, 'You lot are like one big happy family, all taking the piss out of each other! It's magical! I don't really want to go home – can I stay?'

I tend to always wear the same style of clothes on *The Repair Shop*. I like a smart shirt, cuff-links, a waistcoat or jacket and a flat cap. I get my style philosophy from Jeff Goldblum in the eighties sci-fi movie *The Fly*.

In one scene in that film, Jeff opens his wardrobe door and you see five identical suits hanging up. A puzzled Geena Davis asks him: 'Five sets of exactly the same clothes?' And Jeff says: 'Yep. This way, I don't have to expend my thoughts on what I have to wear next.'

I agree. If I wear the same thing every day, I don't have to worry about what to put on. By the same token, I eat the same handful of meals all the time: scrambled eggs, salmon, chicken Caesar salad or a burger. I guess you could call me Groundhog Jay!

Yet, joking aside, there's a serious rationale behind what I wear on *The Repair Shop*. Middle England loves the show, and that's great, but my many years in this country have taught me that some elements of Middle England have always felt wary of black people.

I heard Leona Lewis tell a story on TV that resonated with me. Leona said that she had recently been in a designer clothes shop on the King's Road in London. She was with her father, who is six feet four inches tall and a very well-built guy.

A saleswoman had not recognized Leona and was abrupt and rude to her. She as good as accused her of being there to steal stuff. Leona was upset and had a go at the woman, but her dad jumped in, was placatory to her and smoothed things over.

When they got outside the shop, Leona angrily asked her dad why he had backed down to the woman. And her dad answered: *'I have to make myself small in a lot of situations.'*

I know exactly what he means by that. I know a lot of older viewers who love me on *The Repair Shop* would have crossed the road to avoid me if they'd seen me coming down the street towards them a few years ago. They believe the social trope of the angry, dangerous black man.

If those people saw me on *The Repair Shop* towering over people and looking menacing all in black, as if I was about to film a rap video, it would confirm their prejudices. So, I dress smart and tidy. I dress in an unthreatening way, like their grandads dressed in the thirties.

It's not enough for some people. Most viewers love *The Repair Shop* but I get some negativity on the show's social media. One question haunts me: *Why doesn't Jay Blades do anything? All he does is pass the work on to the others – why doesn't he mend anything?*

Well, the answer is: because that's what the producers ask me to do, and because I'm good at greeting people and helping them to tell their stories. But that doesn't stop the online criticism.

I tend not to read the nasty comments because I try to stay away from negativity. It's like a virus than can infect you and destroy your psyche and, in any case, normally loads of the show's fans leap in to defend me.

At first, the other *Repair Shop* experts got quite upset about me being slagged off online and said it was racist. I tried to rubbish their fears. 'Nah!' I told them. 'It's because I'm the foreman here, dishing out the work, and *nobody* likes a foreman! I don't think it's racist!'

'Oh, yeah?' one of them answered. 'What about Nick Knowles on *DIY SOS*, then? He has exactly the same role that you do, and *he* doesn't get these comments!' And, I must admit, that made me wonder.

Ultimately, though, it's a handful of keyboard warriors out of the five million people who watch *The Repair Shop* now it has moved to a peak-time slot. *And what can you do about them?* I tell the others: 'At least they're watching the show. They're putting our ratings up!'

It's more significant to me that *The Repair Shop* is a genuinely diverse show. Right from the off, I told Ricochet we had to mix things up and have a female upholsterer; a female camera operator; a black camera operator. They've made those things happen. They've been great.

It's true what that magazine editor said: *The Repair Shop* is one great big happy family, onscreen and off. And I'm not going to let a few racist haters dilute that joy for me. Why should I?

Because it's not my problem. It's theirs.

The success of *The Repair Shop* has brought a lot of changes to my life and the biggest one is that it has turned me into what the gossip mags call a celebrity. I get recognized as I walk down the street nowadays and it takes me longer to get places than it used to.

It's funny: it reminds me of when I was doing Street Dreams and Out of the Dark, when Jade would keep me in the house because she knew if I went out, I'd be gone for hours because everybody would want to talk to me! Only now it happens everywhere, not just in High Wycombe!

I'm fine with it. I'm happy to film a message on somebody's phone saying hello to their nan, because she's ninety-six and loves *The Repair Shop* but she can't get out nowadays. I love to chat. It's easy, it makes people happy: where's the problem?

People who stop me ask me questions about *The Repair Shop*, and they usually tend to be the same:

Where do you film the show? (Chichester)
Do you guys really all get on? (Yes)
Do people have to pay to bring stuff in? (No)
Why don't you do any repairs yourself? (Aargh!)

When the media decide that you're a celebrity, of course, you get asked to do celebrity-type stuff. And one of those activities is being invited to guest on other people's television shows.

I didn't want to do *Celebrity Masterchef* when I first got asked. I was too busy and I never cook, except for the same three or four dishes that I make for myself on a loop. But Christine watches the show, and she kept telling me 'Come on, you've got to do it!' Eventually, I gave in.

It became clear just how little I cook when somebody from *Masterchef* phoned me up for a preliminary chat. The conversation basically went like this:

'What's your favourite dish, Jay?'

'Scrambled eggs.'

'If you had a date coming around – what would you cook her?'

'Scrambled eggs with spring onions.'

'*Hmm*. How about if it were a super-important date?'

'Scrambled eggs, spring onions, garlic . . . and something green on top?'

'OK. You're hired!'

I didn't give the show any thought beforehand. In the weeks leading up to it, I was filming *The Repair Shop* and going up and down the country for *Money for Nothing*. I was busy, busy, busy, and I didn't have time to do any practice. Not that I probably would have done, anyway.

I had never even seen *Masterchef*, and Christine suggested that it might be a good idea to watch the show at least once before I went on it. Full of my characteristic inexplicable self-confidence, I declared that I didn't need to.

'It's TV!' I said. 'I know how it'll work! I'll start cooking some stuff, then they'll turn the cameras off and somebody will come out and cook it for me! They'll knock it out and pretend that I have done it!'

Christine looked doubtful. 'Um, I don't think that's how it works, Jay . . .'

'Trust me!' I assured her. 'You don't know TV like I do!'

I was on the show with Clara Amfo from Radio 1 and AJ, the dancer from *Strictly Come Dancing*. Before the first show, we were chatting in the green room, and I asked AJ if he could cook.

'No, mate, not really,' he said. 'I can get by doing stuff like beans on toast, you know?'

Ah, good! I thought. *Somebody else who's on my level!*

We were waiting for hours on the first day so I was a bit anxious when we finally got into the kitchen. Gregg and John, the hosts, greeted us and gave us the task in hand.

'In front of you all is a box,' they told us. 'Underneath it there are some ingredients, and you have one hour to cook a meal out of those ingredients. *Go!*'

The clock started ticking and everyone began running around. AJ went zipping past me looking for something or other. I stood there, holding my box, waiting for someone to say 'Cut!' and a professional chef to step in and cook the meal for me.

I waited . . . and waited . . . and waited. And a terrible truth dawned on me:

Shit, they're not going to say 'Cut!' I've got to cook this thing after all!

I was making fish for my dish, like Cass had taught me. I looked down at the food under my box. I didn't even know what most of the things *were*, but to my relief I saw a bit of fish sticking out.

Right! I'll have that!

I found some tinfoil in a drawer next to me and wrapped the fish in it. I needed chopped-up peppers and onions so I went to a store cupboard and started rooting around. *Bollocks! There's nothing here!* I must have looked a bit frantic because one of the hosts, John, came over to me.

'Are you OK, Jay?' he asked.

'I'm looking for onions and peppers!'

'Oh, you need to go to the market.'

What? I looked at him like he was insane. 'I ain't got time to go to no market!' I said. 'We're filming a show! And I've only got an hour!'

To John's credit, he kept a very straight face. 'No, there's a room over there that we call the market, Jay,' he said, pointing at a door. 'You'll find everything you need in there.'

D'oh! Christine was right! I really should have watched this show before I came on!

I ran to the market and picked up some sweet potatoes and red and green peppers. I wanted yellow peppers as well but they didn't have any, so I took even more red ones. I chopped them up and put them in with the fish.

I don't like catchphrases and I steer clear of them on *The Repair Shop* but for some reason – probably nerves – I developed one on *Celebrity Masterchef*. 'There's my fish ready to cook – bosh!' I told the cameras filming me. 'Now I'm going to make an onion gravy – bosh!'

'Bosh?!' Why was I saying that? I'm not Jamie Oliver! But, for some reason, I couldn't stop!

I was chopping up more and more red peppers – or, so I thought. What I *didn't* know what that I was actually cutting up chillies. I was piling more and more of them into the fish. John came wandering over again.

'How are you doing, Jay?'

'I'm alright!' I said, hopefully. 'There's a bit of pressure, but I think I've got it under control.'

'You might want to scrape some of those seeds out?' he suggested.

Eh? By now I was cutting up more peppers to add to the gravy. I still had no idea they were red-hot chillies. John took a pepper off me, scraped the seeds out on to my chopping board, and walked off.

Huh! I've no idea what he is chatting about! I thought to myself. And I tipped all of the seeds right back into the gravy.

When the dish was cooked, I had to give it to the judges to taste. Gregg Wallace took a bite and looked right surprised. I think he might even have winced.

'Have *you* tasted this dish, Jay?' he asked.

'Yeah!' I told him. 'It's great!'

'It's *very* spicy!' he said. 'Do you always use chillies instead of sweet peppers?'

Damn! As soon as Gregg said it, I realized there were chillies in the fish, the sweet potatoes *and* the gravy! There must have been six of them in there! I'm surprised Gregg didn't have steam coming out of both ears.

'Er, yeah, I like it super-spicy!' I grinned.

I noticed that AJ, who had claimed that he could hardly cook beans on toast, had rustled up a proper Gordon Ramsay-style spread. His meal looked like a masterpiece. He had done the thing I hadn't bothered to do: *practised.*

This wasn't going well. And things were about to get worse.

After they'd tasted our dishes, we had to go back to our benches for the judges' verdicts. Without thinking, I rubbed my face with my hands. *Ouch!* I hadn't washed my hands after I'd been cooking. Meaning my hands were covered in bits of chilli.

As I stood listening to Gregg and John, I felt my face getting hotter and hotter. I felt like I was burning up. I glanced over at AJ and Clara.

'Bloody hot in here, innit?' I asked them.

'Not really,' said AJ. 'You alright, Jay? Your face is well red!'

That chilli was really messing me up! The next time the director said 'Cut', I snuck off to the nearest sink, squirted loads of blue soap over my hands and turned the tap on to wash my hands and face. Nothing came out.

Aargh! The water is turned off! This is a disaster!

We had to film a scene together next. I was stood between AJ and Clara with blue Smurf hands and a beetroot-red face. It wasn't a good look! Miraculously, though, I wasn't eliminated from the show. Somebody had contrived to cook a dish even worse than my super-spicy fish.

Getting through to the next round presented a new problem, though. Namely: *I didn't know any more dishes to cook.* I've got a cousin, Stacey, in Clapton who makes a wicked curry. I asked her to show me how she does it, so I could make it on TV.

Stacey promised to do it the day before the next show, but then had to bail out that morning. *Shit! Now what do I do?* Jade and I were properly back on good terms by now, so I called her. She told me what to buy to make a chicken dish, and said she'd talk me through the recipe on the phone later.

Celebrity Masterchef put me up in a hotel in Whitechapel the night before the second show. My room had a kitchen, so I went to the supermarket, bought all the ingredients Jade told me I needed and headed back to practise. I turned the oven on.

Nothing happened.

What's wrong with this bloody thing?

Damn, it's broken! I'm jinxed!

I raced down to the hotel reception and explained my problem. Could I be moved to a different room? 'I'm sorry, sir,' the smiling receptionist explained. 'We are fully booked!'

'Can I do a bit of cooking in the main hotel kitchen then, please?' I begged. 'It's kind of an emergency!'

The woman made a couple of phone calls and came back shaking her head. 'I'm afraid not,' she told me. 'We're not insured for that.'

It meant that I turned up for *Celebrity Masterchef* round two the next day having never even cooked my chicken dish *once* before. As you'd expect, it was an utter fiasco. I had no idea what I was doing . . . and no amount of saying 'Bosh!' could cover up the fact.

When I'd finished, I basically presented Gregg and John

with a plate of raw chicken. Had they taken one bite, they would have been whisked off to A&E with salmonella poisoning. So that was that. I was out. And that was the end of my *Celebrity Masterchef* adventure.

As game as ever for a new experience, I guested on another couple of programmes. I went on a quiz show called *Richard Osman's House of Games* and found I was well out of my depth. In fact, I was even more out of my comfort zone than I was on *Celebrity Masterchef*. I finished last. *Very* last.

Contestants had to react quickly to words on a screen. This was not a game for dyslexics! I couldn't read the questions, let alone know the answers. One round flashed up letters corresponding to song lyrics. It looked like alphabet soup to me! I don't think I pressed my buzzer once.

I still enjoyed it but, if I am honest, I had more fun on *Would I Lie to You?* Rob Brydon hosted this game show, where contestants on each team had to give conflicting statements. The members of the opposing team had to work out who was telling the truth and who was lying.

I was a plausible liar – I had improved since I was a kid, getting found out for cheating on my girlfriends! – but the star of the show was Bob Mortimer. Bob gave such epic answers that the recording took four hours instead of the normal two. Bob was so funny that I was *willing* his answers to be true!

Away from my TV activities, life in Wolverhampton was good. I was still running Jay & Co from the room in Gerald's warehouse, but by now I had five or six people working for me, the furniture was piling up and we had outgrown the space.

I was doing some community work on the side mentoring artists and craftspeople in the Maws Craft Centre in Ironbridge in Shropshire, twenty miles from Wolverhampton. Ironbridge is a lovely historic town that gets a lot of tourists, but they weren't visiting the craft centre.

I explained to the artists how they could use social media and work as a collective to pull in more footfall. Then they showed me some buildings they were renovating. One was a whitewashed former Victorian school. It was a lovely old space that was now standing empty and I fell bang in love with it.

'Could I rent this one?' I asked them. They said that would be fine, and *voila*! Suddenly, Jay & Co had a beautiful, spacious new headquarters. I was delighted.

Between my TV work and Jay & Co, I was firing on all cylinders at the end of 2019. I was a proper busy worker bee, which is how I like it, and I saw no reason why the following year shouldn't be the same but even more so.

I turned fifty in February 2020 and threw a big party. I chose a highly symbolic venue. Back in the sixties, Wolverhampton had been the Parliamentary constituency of Enoch Powell, a Conservative government minister who was virulently anti-immigration.

In 1968, two years before I was born, Powell had made a controversial speech predicting 'rivers of blood' flowing through the streets of Britain if immigration from the British Commonwealth was not checked. His inflammatory words arguably triggered the rise of the National Front and the racial hatred I suffered as a teenager in Hackney.

Powell used to frequent a social club in Wolverhampton

that was now known as the Heritage Club – and that was where I decided to hold my fiftieth bash. There were no rivers of blood flowing, but plenty of lakes of lager and wine!

The night felt special. Against all the odds, here I was, living life to the full, defying the teachers in my secondary school, the racist bullies, even the social media trolls. Despite all of those haters . . . I was making it.

My BBC colleagues from *The Repair Shop* and *Money for Nothing* came, as did old muckers from the past and my Wolverhampton crew. My mum flew in from Barbados. It was a fantastic night and I felt on top of the world and ready for whatever came next.

Or so I thought. How wrong I was! The next month dawned, and . . . *bosh*! Out of the blue, the world suddenly came to a halt and closed down.

14

The Repair Shop is always open . . .

I'VE SEEN A FEW THINGS IN MY LIFE BY NOW AND I LIKE to think that it takes a lot to surprise me. Like everybody else, though, I have been completely knocked backwards by the coronavirus pandemic that at time of writing has claimed over two million lives across the world.

It's been totally extraordinary. Nobody has known what to do because there has been no precedent in our lifetime. We're not used to mass diseases that wipe out whole swathes of the population and bring everyday life as we have always known it to a juddering halt.

Who would have thought, at the start of 2020, that we'd spend most of the next eighteen months unable to see our loved ones, not allowed even to stand next to each other, scurrying through deserted streets in face masks? It's been like living in a bad science-fiction movie that goes on and on.

Covid has put a stop to everything for a lot of people, but I'm aware that I'm lucky. I can still be a solitary worker bee in a pandemic. I can escape to Jay & Co's workshop in Ironbridge and beaver away on my own fixing my furniture. I can just lock the door and get on with it.

Television is a different matter. The first full lockdown wiped out any chance of filming a new series of *The Repair Shop* in spring 2020 and the TV and production companies had to scramble to fill the gaps in the TV schedules. They had to think on their feet – and they did.

I made two new shows at Jay & Co. The BBC sent a socially-distanced cameraman to stand two metres away from me and film me making *Jay Blades' Home Fix*. It showed people who don't even know which way up to hold a hammer how to do basic DIY while they were locked down.

Ricochet repackaged existing footage from old episodes of *The Repair Shop* into a spin-off series called *The Repair Shop: Fixing Britain*. This was an interesting show that compiled various old repairs along themes such as music, engineering and immigration.

The immigration episode was great. We revisited items such as the old pump organ as we talked about the *Windrush* generation facing racism here and emphasized how much colour, vitality and variety immigrants from all over the world have brought to Britain over the decades.

It struck a chord with me, as did another episode about World War II. It was a second chance to see Steve mend a watch that a Dutch lady had hidden, sewn in her clothes, for four years after the Japanese herded her into a POW camp in Indonesia. Her grandson had brought it in to us.

Yet the focus on World War II reminded me of my

university days and how I had learned there of Indian, African and Caribbean soldiers who had fought alongside the Allied troops. Sometimes they were used as cannon fodder and sent as advance troops against the Nazis' guns.

Those brave guys made just as big a sacrifice as their white colleagues in arms, and yet they are written out of history and never mentioned whenever D-Day anniversary celebrations come around. You'd think the war was won purely by white soldiers. It really, really wasn't.

We needed to do new voiceovers for the *Fixing Britain* compilations. Normally the well-known actor Bill Paterson narrates *The Repair Shop* in his lovely Scottish burr, but for this spin-off show the producers decided that they fancied a change. They wanted me to do it.

I was flattered – but it also presented me with a problem. *How could I read a script, with my dyslexia?* The average *Fixing Britain* voiceover, on paper, was twenty-five pages long. I'm not joking when I say it would take me days, *weeks* to read that! How could we make it work?

The only way was for me to listen to the script via my trusty Dragon computer software, attempt to memorize it and then get as close to it as I could. It was a challenging process initially, and one producer who was working with me remotely couldn't get her head around it.

'Why don't you just *read* it?' she asked me, bluntly.

'Because I can't read,' I explained. 'I listen to it, then I repeat it.'

'That's insane!' she marvelled. 'How do you *do* that?' But once I got into the groove, I was able to do the voiceovers fairly well.

The Ricochet guys sent me some gear then video-called

me and told me how to set up a makeshift studio next to a sink in my workshop. I stood in that tiny space and narrated the whole series as the producers and sound guys coaxed me along remotely. We got there. Eventually!

We had the occasional hitch, mind. One day I had memorized a section of script and was just reciting it back when the engineer interrupted me.

'There's some rustling on the line, Jay,' he said. 'Any idea what it is?'

'No,' I admitted.

'It might be your clothes,' he speculated. 'Can you take off your shirt?'

'OK!' I did, but the rustling persisted. The sound guy was baffled. 'Are you wearing another shirt?'

'Yeah, I had a t-shirt under my shirt.'

'Right, take that off as well. You're the only person there, aren't you?'

'Yeah, I am. Alright, will do!' I whipped off my t-shirt, which seemed to solve the noise problem. I continued happily narrating away for twenty minutes and was totally immersed in the voiceover when a knock came at the door.

It was a customer to collect a chair. I handed it over and we had a bit of a chinwag. She gave me a funny look, as did her hubby who'd come to help her to carry it. I had no idea why, until I closed the door behind them, caught sight of myself in a mirror and did a cartoon double-take.

Jay! You bloody muppet! That nice couple must think that you spend all day in here restoring furniture half-naked! It was proper embarrassing.

While I was locked down in my old schoolhouse, with just two hundred chairs for company, it gave me a lot of time, and good cause, to think back over my life to date for this book – where I started from, and my rollercoaster, up-and-down journey to where I am now. *My repair job.*

I got together with a ghost-writer, Ian, we talked about my life in detail for weeks and he helped me to get it down on paper in this book. I often found myself shaking my head in amazement. *Wow, what a life I've had so far!*

And then in June, as the government lifted lockdown restrictions for a while, I went to a couple of events that emphasized two extremes of that life.

Four months after my own half-century, my old school-mate DJ Spoony celebrated his fiftieth birthday with a spectacularly lavish affair. On a Sunday afternoon, he threw a party, livestreamed across social media, aimed at celebrating black excellence and raising money for charity.

I went down to the event in London. It was well slick. Hackney-boy-made-good Idris Elba was there, as were Trevor Nelson, Ian Wright and Reggie Yates. Guest of honour was Baroness Doreen Lawrence, whose son, Stephen, was infamously murdered in Eltham in 1993.

It's always good to see Spoony and his party was a sophisticated event but I didn't stick around there too long. Because I had another, very much more low-key bash to go to.

On the same day, another old mate from my schooldays, a cool guy named Winston Adams, had also invited me to his fiftieth. I was keen to go because I knew I'd see a lot of the old faces from when I was a kid.

It was thirty people in a park in Tottenham – well, 'park' is flattering it! It was a patch of wasteland, really, with fast-food boxes and crap lying around everywhere. Winston had paper plates of fish, chicken, coleslaw and cake balanced on a wall, and his guests were drinking lager out of paper cups. He was certainly keeping it real!

It was rough and ready and messy and I absolutely loved it. It was all of my yesterdays. There were so many friends I remembered from the old estate, and as we got talking and reminiscing, the memories came flooding back like a tidal wave . . .

'Hey, Jay, remember when you got run out of Stoke Newington? That guy was going to kill you, bruv!'

'Shit, what about the time you tried to fight Islington in a woman's dressing gown?'

'Have you still got your rounders bat, Batman?'

We had a million stories to tell. A million memories to share. We had all changed, yet we were still the same people. Just being with these guys again was so powerful and emotional. And then, to my embarrassment, they started lavishing praise on me.

'Jay, you're the first one of us that's made it out of here!' one of them said. 'You're back with us right now but, in life, you're *up there!*'

'No, I'm not!' I replied. 'Look at me! I'm still the same as you!'

'You are, but you're *not*, bruv! We see you on TV! You're a black geezer and you've got shows on the BBC, man! We're all so proud of you!'

Wow! It was intense and it was overwhelming. I was having so much love poured over me by these guys from back in the day, that I had run with for years, that I couldn't handle it. *It was too much.* I did what I did when I sat with Gerald Bailey in his car after my breakdown.

265

I started crying.

'Fucking shut up, you lot!' I sniffled at them. 'I only came here to have a bit of cake, a little drink and a reminisce, and now you're fucking me up! Leave me alone!'

But I was smiling through my tears. Thirty years ago, if you'd told me I'd be happy crying in front of all my mates from the estate, my guys from the ghetto, I'd have thought you were mad. I'd probably have smacked you one! Now, it felt incredible.

We talked about the good times *and* the bad. We shared the old horror stories of Blackbeard, and of being pulled off the streets into police vans and getting kicked to shit. And as I drove back to Wolverhampton the next day, I wondered just how much has changed.

I had got talking to Doreen Lawrence at Spoony's party. The black community see her as our mother, and I thanked her for fighting for us and for continuing the never-ending struggle against racial inequality. Her reply was humbling.

'I'm just like all black mums, Jay,' she said. 'That's what we do. Full stop. I just happen to be in the limelight, so people can hear me.'

'What do you think the future holds?' I asked her. 'We've been fighting the same battles all of our lives – *how do we sort this problem out?*' The sad thing was that Doreen didn't have an answer. She doesn't know.

Don't get me wrong. I'm not saying there is no hope. I appreciate the Black Lives Matter movement. It's the first time in my life that I've seen black people, white people, Chinese, Turks, *everybody* coming together as one to say, 'No, this is wrong!' You have to welcome that.

At the same time, I wonder: how much is *really* going to

change? Look at the reality. Look at the demographics. At the time of writing it's 2021 and I'm the first – no, the *only* – black geezer hosting a light entertainment TV show in Britain. How can that make sense? How can that be right?

I don't want to get on a soapbox here, but I look at society and I see the same things I saw twenty years ago, when I wrote a university dissertation called *Manufacturing a Black Criminal*. I see the over-representation of young black men in prison. I see them being excluded from schools.

You go to Hackney now, or Brixton, and they are super-gentrified but they still have pockets of deprivation. Those are where the black people live. When I walk around Brixton, I see hip bars where the only black people are the security guards who are there to keep the locals out.

I see bad policing and stop-and-search still going on. A black MP, Dawn Butler, got stopped in August 2020. Just a month earlier, a black athlete, Bianca Williams, who has won medals for Great Britain at the Commonwealth Games, got put in handcuffs while she was in her car with her partner and their baby boy.

It's all still going on. And it's all still wrong.

That shit scars you and it's impossible to ignore. I'm on *The Repair Shop* now so Middle England accepts me. People don't lock their car doors as I walk past any more – they want a selfie instead! It's lovely, but I can't forget the forty-five years when I was made to feel I didn't belong in England.

But I'm all about positivity, not negativity, so I try to do what I can. I can see why there are a lot of angry black people about, because I used to be one – *sometimes, I still am!* – but the problem with anger is it can drive people away. So, I try to take a different tack.

On my social media, I have launched Sunday School. I post each Sunday, celebrating black historic figures who have contributed to the fabric of Britain. I think there have been a few surprises there and I've been really pleased by the response.

In Sunday School, I've spoken about Mary Seacole, the British-Jamaican nurse who tended to wounded soldiers in the Crimean war. I've talked about Septimius Severus, the African-born Roman emperor who came to Britain, strengthened Hadrian's Wall, and is buried in York.

I've also talked about Dr Harold Moody, who came over from Jamaica in 1904 to study medicine, set up his own practice when he couldn't get work and founded the League of Coloured People. And I gave a plug to Professor Stuart Hall, whose teachings on criminology I loved so much at university.

They are black figures who many people will not have heard of but they all made deep, profound contributions to British life and society. And I hope that every time somebody new learns about them, and people like them, one more little piece of prejudice and bigotry will fall away.

Because it really should.

After my incredibly moving night at Winston's birthday party in east London, I drove back up to Wolverhampton with a million thoughts flying around my head. And as I settled back into restoring chairs at Jay & Co, another phantom from my past re-emerged.

I get all sorts of strange phone calls in Ironbridge.

People phone me up with all kinds of weird requests. So, at first, it didn't seem anything out of the ordinary when my workshop phone rang late one afternoon.

'Do you restore paintings?' the bloke asked when I picked up.

'No, mate, I don't.'

'Oh,' he said. 'Well, it's not really the painting that needs mending. It's the frame.'

There was something odd about this call. Something familiar about the voice. But I couldn't put my finger on it.

'If it's a nice frame, you need to get in touch with an art restorer,' I told him.

There was a pause.

'You don't know who this is, do you?' he asked.

I didn't. And then, suddenly, a split second before he told me, *I did.*

'It's your father,' he said.

'Wait . . . what?' It was all I could think of to say. 'Really?'

'Yes.'

Another pause. Then, The Man Who Contributed Towards My Birth spoke to me again. *And what he said knocked me sideways.*

'Jay, everything you are doing is down to me.'

Wow! I was lost for words.

'Is it?' I asked.

'Yes, of course! I am a carpenter! *That* is how you have your ability!'

Oh. My. Days. Was I really hearing this right? But I could see where this conversation might be heading. And I wasn't going to let it get there.

'What is it you want?' I asked him.

'What do you mean?'

'I mean, what do you want? I haven't heard from you in thirty years. So why are you ringing me *now*? What do you want from me?'

A deafening silence came down the line.

'Really, what do you want?' I persisted. 'You ain't never given me nothing in my life and now *you* must want something. Well, what is it?'

I could hear TMWCTMB breathing hard, but he still wasn't speaking. So, I summarized where he and I stood before I hung up on him.

I told him I've only learned one thing from him: how not to be a father. I've tried my whole life not to follow in his footsteps. I haven't always succeeded, or been the most brilliant dad in the world, but I love my kids more than anything and I provide for all of them. And I'm as proud of that as I am of anything I've achieved.

I guess I've never expected anything from TMWCTMB, and he's never let me down on that score . . . yet he *did* give me something recently. Naturally, it was completely accidental and unintended.

He gave me back my elder sister. The one he always told me doesn't exist.

TMWCTMB must be a little bit proud of me, I guess, because he'd apparently been boasting around northwest London that he has a son who is on telly. He is friends with Samantha's uncle, who told her about it. Samantha put two and two together, worked out that I must be her half-brother, and called me.

It was such a thrill to hear from her. *Samantha! The only one of my twenty-five siblings who is older than me – and the one I have longed to see again ever since our sole meeting, forty-five years ago!*

She has done great in life. After her mum's fling with TMWCTMB, she went on to marry an African business-man who later became sports commissioner for Nigeria. Samantha went to private school and then became a creative working in the broadcast media industry. That's what she is doing now.

Wow! She and I have spoken and exchanged texts. I'm excited to be in touch and I can't wait to meet her again. We haven't done so yet, because I've been full on with *The Repair Shop* and because of Covid lockdowns, but when we do, it's going to be wonderful.

We have a lot of catching up to do, and I want to do it properly.

Having Samantha back in my life is great, and at the same time I'm totally focused on the family that I've always had. Levi, Dior and Zola are very different yet they are all doing great. I'm so proud of them.

Levi is a worker bee for the water board in Bedford, on the road fixing pipes all day. Dior still dances to his own tune and can still charm the birds from the trees. He is training to be an engineer, but what he really wants is a career in music. I think he'll get it.

Zola has just got into the National Youth Theatre and is staying with her mum in Turkey. Jade moved back there a few months ago. Zola is currently studying remotely because of the virus, so she went with her. It's great: Zola is half-Turk-ish, so it's important she understands Turkish culture.

Jade and Zola are in Turkey yet Jade's mum is here. Jade's parents got divorced a few years ago and her mum,

Heather, moved back to High Wycombe. Every couple of months, I make time to call her and check she is OK (and, Covid permitting, take her out for lunch).

I see my second parents, Cass and Thelma, all the time. I always take Thelma flowers. She asks her boys, Gerald and Pie: 'Why do *you* never bring me flowers? Jay is my only son that does it! What is *wrong* with you two?' She busts their balls about it, and I laugh my head off.

Thelma sometimes says that God sent me to her and Cass. Well, if He is up there, I know that He certainly sent them to me, just at a time that I desperately needed them! Those two, and Gerald, saved my life. I will love them forever.

My mum has been back in Barbados for twenty-five years now and she is happy there. *She ain't never coming back here – full stop!* I go over there to see her every two or three years, and each time I understand better why she loves it there so much.

I step off the plane in Barbados and the very *air* of the island feels therapeutic. I feel my shoulders relax, and I start to breathe more easily and freely. If I am honest, it is where I feel I belong. It feels more like home than England has at any point in my life.

I'm pretty sure that I'll go back to Barbados to live when I'm an old geezer. I won't need a big house. I'll just get myself a little hut, ideally somewhere near to the beach, and I'll live off the land. That blissful, chilled life will be idyllic. A dream.

I'm not going just yet, though. Because I still have too much to do here.

*

The Repair Shop is back in full swing and I'm still loving doing it. Mind you, it's a bit of a ball-ache filming during coronavirus. All of the items that people bring in have to be sanitized and quarantined for seventy-two hours before we can do anything with them.

The restorers and I do what we call our Covid Dance. When I take them an item, they have to step back from their bench while I put it in the middle. Then I step back as they take it. Production staff are standing by to squirt sanitizer in our hands. It's a right palaver.

The worst part is not being able to touch our guests. I love to step out and give them a sympathetic hug when they get tearful, but now we can't go within two metres of them. So, as I haven't got Mr Tickle arms, it's a no-no.

We're still getting great items and great stories. A lady, Michelle, came in with her grandmother's wedding ring. She said that back in the day, her gran had been engaged to be married, and went off to the pub one evening to meet her fiancé.

While she was waiting for him, she met another guy in there. She was smitten from the second she set eyes on him. She dumped her fiancé and married the new guy – wow, talk about love at first sight! And *here was her ring*. So much human joy, and passion, and history in one little gold band!

There's something about *The Repair Shop* that whisks me back to my time of innocence, before I became aware of racism, turned to fighting and the start of the bad times. It takes me back to Cazenove Road, and playing British Bulldog and Kick the Can. And recently an item zoomed me right back to the heart of my childhood.

A lady, Joyce, came in with her grandad's battered old

bag that he used to carry his crown-green bowling balls in. *Whoosh*! The second I saw it, I was whisked back to Springfield Park in Hackney, where I used to go with my cousins to play on the swings and pick blackberries.

There was a bowling green in the park. I didn't understand the rules, but I used to peer through the hedge at all of the old geezers and women playing it and think, *Wow, that looks cool! I'm going to play that game one day!*

I totally forgot that thought, and that green, and that game as I grew up and got urbanized, but the minute the lady walked in *The Repair Shop* door with the bag, it all came flooding back to me. Suddenly, I was that kid again, peering through that hedge!

I listened to her story about her grandad intently, nodding along. 'Yeah, cool! I am going to learn how to bowl!' I told her. I looked around to see sceptical expressions on the faces of the team. Their thoughts weren't exactly hard to read:

You what?! Jay, man, you're a black guy from the mean streets of Hackney! You've got a gold tooth! What the hell are you going on about, you are going to learn crown-green bowling?!

Yet as I carried on enthusing, I saw their expressions change: *No, he means it! He's for real! He's not acting!* I've already spoken to a guy about getting bowling balls and being measured for a jacket. Joining a Wolverhampton crown-green bowling club is high on my to-do list.

The BBC have just renewed *The Repair Shop* for three more years and I think it's going to be like the *Antiques Roadshow*. It's just going to go on and on for ever and ever. I am grateful, and I want to be on it for a long time yet, but I'm also interested in doing other things.

I don't mean more celebrity reality shows! You can forget seeing me on *I'm A Celebrity . . . Get Me Out of Here!* I'm not going to the jungle: I hate bugs. As for *Strictly Come Dancing*: I don't really think the nation needs to see my meat-and-two-veg packed into Lycra on a Saturday teatime!

No, I'm more interested in making shows that can make a big difference to people's lives. Leigh-Anne from Little Mix approached me when she was making a documentary about racism in the music industry. She has suffered from it along the way, and she wanted to ask my advice about how we can try to change the narrative.

I was proud and honoured to be involved, and I'm working out a few ideas for future projects. I can't say much right now, but . . . watch this space.

I've got six young people working with me at Jay & Co, and every day I juggle my furniture business alongside my TV work. As I've got busier and busier, I've had to learn to delegate more. It can be challenging but, in a funny way, I take inspiration from Alexander McQueen.

McQueen has been dead for more than ten years but he is still bringing out two collections a year! He does catwalk shows from the grave! The point is that the business wasn't just him, just as Jay & Co isn't just me. I have learned that the Co is just as important as the Jay.

I still guide the ship, though. When I get a break from filming at *The Repair Shop*, I'll often be sitting looking at photos that my young guys have texted to me of furniture they have spotted at auctions or in second-hand shops. I ping them messages back:

Yes, buy that one!

No, don't get that one!

Ever since Street Dreams and Out of the Dark, I've felt as if my calling is to help young people. I still have my dream of becoming the Jamie Oliver of furniture.

In the same way that Jamie did his Fifteen restaurant, I'd like to launch the Jay & Co Academy to teach kids how to restore old furniture – and more! Just like High Wycombe was Britain's centre of furniture, there are parts of the country that have vast histories of making shoes, or lace, or cotton.

I'd love to set up academies in those towns where retirees from those industries could train up youngsters in their crucial skills, just like Jade and I did with Out of the Dark. It's such an exciting idea. I want to make it happen.

I'm leading a crazily busy life nowadays but I am happy with it, happy with where I am, what I am and *who I am*. I've sussed that I'm a communicator, and that I'm most contented when I'm helping people in life. Those are the things I'm destined to do.

Today, I'm on the right Scalextric track and I'm still whizzing around at speed, but I know I need to give myself a bit of care and attention every now and then. I have to take my car off the track, dust it down and check the wheels.

Most of all, I have to make sure that I don't come shooting off the track and find myself driving through a tunnel of light again.

I need to remember my personality diagnosis: *I'm an extreme introvert acting like an extrovert*. I know I spend a lot of time out of my comfort zone, and I need to be careful not to stretch myself too far and overdo it like I was doing when I broke myself.

Life is good now. I'm over my breakdown . . . but my repair job is still a work in progress. *It always will be.* I'm like a vase someone brings into *The Repair Shop*. We can fix it up and make it beautiful again, but it only needs your kid to knock it off the shelf and it's smashed into bits again.

The difference now is that, if I break again, I know how to ask for help. I'll have people around me who will recognize the signs and take me to a repair shop. I won't finish up sitting for however many days in a car park, in a city I don't know – even if that city *has* now become the home that I love.

So, what's it all about, Jay?

Ultimately, I've learned, *all you can do is be good.* Put goodness into the universe and karma will give it back to you. That's not a bad rule to live by. It happened to me when I fell apart, and the kindness of near-strangers helped to put me back together again.

This memoir is about *Making It*, and I wouldn't have made it to where I am without those people's help. They taught me the most important life lesson of all: *The Repair Shop* is always open for all of us, and we should never be afraid to check in.